# AMERICA the BEAUTIFUL

# ALASKA

## By Ann Heinrichs

### Consultants

**Douglas A. Phillips,** Social Studies Program Coordinator for the Anchorage School District

**R. N. DeArmond,** Alaska Historian, Juneau

**R. L. Hillerich, Ph.D.,** Bowling Green State University, Bowling Green, Ohio

CHILDRENS PRESS®
CHICAGO

**Climbers on Mount McKinley**

Project Editor: Joan Downing
Associate Editor: Shari Joffe
Design Director: Margrit Fiddle
Typesetting: Graphic Connections, Inc.
Engraving: Liberty Photoengraving

Library of Congress Cataloging-in-Publication Data

Heinrichs, Ann.
  America the beautiful. Alaska / by Ann Heinrichs.
    p.   cm.
  Summary: Discusses the land, people, history,
government, economy, sports, and recreation of
Alaska.
  ISBN 0-516-00448-4
  1.  Alaska—Juvenile literature.  [1.  Alaska.]
I.  Title.
F904.3.H45   1990                          90-33847
979.8—dc20                                 CIP
                                           AC

A Tundra Buggy on a polar bear tour

## TABLE OF CONTENTS

# Chapter 1
# THE LAST FRONTIER

# THE LAST FRONTIER

Called the Great Land by its Aleut natives, Alaska is a land of great extremes. The nation's largest state, it has both the highest mountain and the largest glacier in North America. Its volcano chain is the longest in the world.

Alaska offers a richness and diversity found in few other states. The land itself ranges from lush rain forest to treeless Arctic plain. From its rugged landscape rise fuming volcanoes, glistening glaciers, and lofty mountain peaks. Brilliant wildflowers blaze across the tundra, while spruce and hemlock shelter the shadowy forest floor.

Alaska's wildlife is as diverse as its land. Giant brown bears fish the streams for salmon, and herds of caribou roam the mountains and plains. Along coastal waterways are regal bald eagles and snub-nosed puffins, fur seals and killer whales.

This wild and robust land lured a rich mix of peoples to its shores. Sustained by hunting and fishing, Alaska's earliest peoples have pursued their traditions for thousands of years. Later arrivals, enticed by Alaska's rich resources, transplanted their cultures from Europe and Asia.

Known as the Last Frontier, Alaska remains sparsely settled and largely untouched. Thousands of fur trappers and gold rushers hacked their way through the wilderness in Alaska's early days; and even now, scores of towns cannot be reached by road. Today, as in the past, it takes a sturdy breed of people to make a life on the Last Frontier.

# Chapter 2
## THE LAND

# THE LAND

## GEOGRAPHY

The state of Alaska is a vast, sprawling expanse of land on the northwest tip of the North American continent. Along with Hawaii, Alaska is one of the two states in the nation that do not share borders with any other states. Alaskans call the United States mainland the Lower 48.

Covering 591,004 square miles (1,530,700 square kilometers), Alaska is the largest state in the Union. It is nearly one-fifth the size of the Lower 48. Texas, the next-largest state, is less than half the size of Alaska. Tiny Rhode Island, the smallest state, would fit into Alaska 480 times!

From Alaska's "body" extend two long "legs"—the Aleutian Islands chain to the southwest and the Panhandle on the southeast. Actually a large peninsula jutting out into the ocean, Alaska is surrounded by water on three sides. To the north is the Arctic Ocean. The Bering Sea separates Alaska's western shores from Siberia, in the Soviet Union. Across a narrow channel called the Bering Strait, only 51 miles (82 kilometers) of water lie between the Alaskan and Soviet mainlands. The Pacific Ocean and the Gulf of Alaska wash Alaska's southern shores. On the east, Alaska borders the Canadian provinces of British Columbia and the Yukon Territory.

**Mineral rich Polychrome Hills in Denali National Park**

A land of diverse and complex land features, Alaska is often divided into six geographic regions: the southeast, Copper River, Cook Inlet, Aleutian, Kuskokwim-Yukon, and Arctic regions.

The southeast consists of Alaska's Panhandle. The Copper River region stretches from Prince William Sound and Malaspina Glacier up through the Copper River basin to the Mentasta Mountains. The Cook Inlet region extends north from Kodiak Island to include Iliamna Lake, Cook Inlet, the Kenai Peninsula, and the Mount McKinley area. The Aleutian Island chain and the Alaska Peninsula belong to the Aleutian region. The vast drainage area of the Kuskokwim and Yukon rivers makes up the Kuskokwim-Yukon region. The Arctic region, north of the Yukon drainage basin up to the Arctic Ocean, includes the Seward Peninsula.

**Rain forests line Alaska's southern Gulf Coast and Panhandle.**

## TOPOGRAPHY

Geologists—scientists who study the earth's mineral and rock formations—usually separate Alaska into four geological land regions: the Pacific Mountain System, the Central Plateau, the Rocky Mountain System, and the Arctic Coastal Plain.

The Pacific Mountain System is part of a string of mountain ranges that extend along the Pacific Coast from southern California to Alaska. Forming an arc along Alaska's southern coast, this chain of peaks stretches from the southeast all the way through the Aleutian Islands. The Saint Elias, Chugach, Wrangell, and Kenai mountains are the major ranges in Alaska's coastal arc. A second arc, farther inland, includes the Aleutian Range, the Alaska Range, and the Coast Mountains. Though the Pacific region is marked by volcanoes, glaciers, and some of North America's highest peaks, its lowlands are known for their forests and rich farmland.

Alaska's Central Plateau covers most of the state's interior. Also called the Central Uplands and Lowlands, it forms a rather low-lying basin between the Brooks Range to the north and the Alaska Range to the south. The Kuskokwim Mountains and other low, rolling ranges vary the plateau's landscape, while boggy land called muskeg covers much of the lowlands. The Yukon and Kuskokwim river systems drain the Central Plateau.

The Rocky Mountain System is an extension of North America's Rocky Mountains. Also called the Arctic Mountain System, it encompasses the peaks and foothills of the Brooks Range. Within this system are the De Long, Baird, Schwatka, Endicott, Philip Smith, Romanzof, and Davidson mountains. The range's peaks are higher in the east than in the west—up to 9,000 feet (2,743 meters).

The Arctic Coastal Plain is a frigid expanse of land that slopes northward from the Brooks Range to the Arctic Ocean. Also called the Arctic Slope, this entire region lies within the Arctic Circle. It is also north of the timberline, meaning that large trees cannot grow there. The land in this large, treeless region is called tundra. Permafrost, or permanently frozen subsoil, ranges from a few feet deep in some places on the tundra to 2,000 feet (610 meters) in others. During the summer, when the permafrost close to the surface thaws, the tundra is carpeted with a thick layer of mosses, wildflowers, and short grasses. Point Barrow, on the Arctic Ocean, is the northernmost point in the United States.

## COASTAL WATERS AND ISLANDS

Alaska's general coastline, measuring 6,640 miles (10,686 kilometers), is longer than the entire seacoast of the Lower 48. The state's total coastline is more than five times as long as its general coast. Counting the shores of all its bays, inlets, and islands, Alaska's coastline measures 33,904 miles (54,562 kilometers).

The waters that wash Alaska's south-central coast are known as the Gulf of Alaska. Cook Inlet cuts a channel between the western side of the Kenai Peninsula and the mainland. Prince William Sound joins the Gulf of Alaska on the peninsula's eastern side. Bristol Bay, Kuskokwim Bay, and Norton Sound flow into the Bering Sea off Alaska's western shores. Both the Chukchi Sea to the northwest and the Beaufort Sea to the northeast are extensions of the northerly Arctic Ocean.

Scattered along Alaska's coast are thousands of islands, rocks, and reefs. Of the eighteen hundred islands that have been given names, about one thousand comprise the Alexander Archipelago in the southeast. Of these, the largest is Prince of Wales Island, followed by Chichagof, Admiralty, Baranof, Revillagigedo, and Kupreanof islands.

The Aleutian Island chain extends 1,600 miles (2,575 kilometers) southwestward into the Pacific Ocean. Unimak is the chain's largest island, followed by Unalaska and Umnak. Cape Wrangell, on the Aleutians' Attu Island, is the westernmost point in the United States.

Kodiak Island, in the Gulf of Alaska, is the state's largest island. The major islands in the Bering Sea are Saint Lawrence, Nunivak, and the Pribilofs.

## RIVERS AND LAKES

More than three thousand rivers wind their way through Alaska's vast interior. The longest, the Yukon, is also the fourth-longest river in North America. Running through Canada for part of its course, the Yukon has a total length of 1,979 miles (3,185

**Kodiak Island is the state's largest island.**

kilometers). It enters Alaska from the Yukon Territory, follows a
northwesterly course to Fort Yukon, and then flows southwest
until it empties into Norton Sound. Several of Alaska's other
important rivers—the Koyukuk, the Tanana, the Innoko, and the
Porcupine—are tributaries of the Yukon.

The Kuskokwim River is Alaska's second-longest river. From its
source in the Alaska Range, it flows southwest to Kuskokwim
Bay, part of the Bering Sea. Important rivers in Alaska's southern
region include the Matanuska and the Susitna rivers, which empty
into Cook Inlet, and the Copper River, flowing from the Wrangell
Mountains to the Gulf of Alaska. The major river in the Arctic
region is the Colville River, which empties into the Arctic Ocean.
Other important Alaskan rivers include the Noatak, Kobuk,
Chilkat, Kvichak, Naknek, Nushagak, and Stikine rivers.

**Portage Glacier, a few miles southeast of Anchorage**

If a map of Alaska were drawn in complete detail, it would show more than three million lakes. Ninety-four of them would have surface areas greater than 10 square miles (26 square kilometers). Lakes are especially numerous around the Yukon and Kuskokwim river deltas and on the Arctic Slope south of Barrow. Iliamna Lake, west of Cook Inlet on the Alaska Peninsula, is the state's largest, measuring more than 1,000 square miles (2,590 square kilometers). Some of Alaska's other large lakes include Becharof, Teshekpuk, Naknek, Tustumena, Clark, and Dall.

## MOUNTAINS, GLACIERS, AND VOLCANOES

Fourteen of Alaska's mountains are higher than any others in the United States. Mount McKinley, in the Alaska Range, is the state's highest peak. Towering 20,320 feet (6,194 meters) over Denali National Park, McKinley is also the tallest mountain in all of North America. Second highest is Mount Saint Elias, measuring 18,008 feet (5,489 meters) high. Other Alaskan peaks, all higher than 15,000 feet (4,572 meters), are Mount Bona, Mount Blackburn, and Mount Sanford, in the Wrangell Mountains;

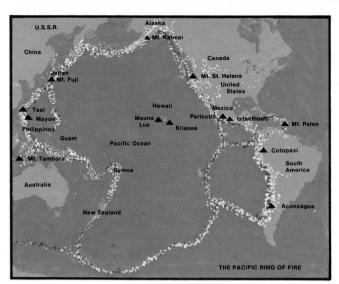

Mount Augustine (above) is one of the volcanoes that is part of the Pacific Ocean's Ring of Fire (left).

Mount Fairweather, in the Chugach Mountains; and Mount Foraker, in the Alaska Range.

Glaciers cover nearly 29,000 square miles (75,110 square kilometers) of Alaskan land—almost 5 percent of the state's total area! In fact, about three-fourths of Alaska's fresh-water supply is in the form of glacial ice. Glaciers are actually sheets of ice that advance, or flow, much as rivers do. They build up over many years, when more snow falls than melts. Glaciers take many forms, some covering valleys or filling basins, others hugging mountainsides or plateaus. When several valley glaciers connect, they form what is called an ice field.

Most of Alaska's 100,000 glaciers are concentrated in the south and the southeast. The largest glacier in Alaska, and in all of North America, is Malaspina, in the Saint Elias Range. Malaspina itself covers 850 square miles (2,202 square kilometers). Counting its tributary glaciers, the Malaspina complex covers about 2,000 square miles (5,180 square kilometers). Bering Glacier is Alaska's longest, extending for more than 100 miles (161 kilometers).

Alaska is also known for having the world's longest chain of active volcanoes. Scattered through the Aleutian Islands, the Alaska Peninsula, and the Wrangell Mountains, these peaks are part of what is called the Pacific Ocean's Ring of Fire. The tallest

Native Alaskan animals and plants include (clockwise from above) Alaskan brown bears, who are excellent salmon catchers; puffins; Arctic tundra wildflowers, shown here in the rosy colors of autumn; and tundra lichen, shown here with flowering dogwood.

volcano is Mount Wrangell, which emits smoke continuously. Mount Spurr, Redoubt Volcano, and Iliamna Volcano are the next tallest.

More than seventy of Alaska's volcanoes are active or potentially active. Redoubt Volcano was spewing ash over south-central Alaska during much of 1990. Pavlof Volcano, with forty-one reported eruptions, sent ash 10 miles (16 kilometers) into the sky during its April 1986 eruption. Mount Veniaminof, on the Alaska Peninsula, erupted almost nonstop from June 1983 to April 1984. Novarupta Volcano's 1912 eruption was the world's largest in the twentieth century.

## PLANTS AND ANIMALS

Although forests cover one-third of the land, there are fewer species of native trees in Alaska than in any other state. Western hemlock and Sitka spruce flourish in the coastal forests. Other timber species include Alaska yellow cedar, red cedar, mountain hemlock, white spruce, lodgepole pine, paper birch, and black cottonwood. On the Alaska Peninsula and the Aleutian Islands, tall grasses grow in place of trees.

Alaska's muskeg bogs support mosses, lichens, cranberries, skunk cabbage, and bog laurel. On the Arctic tundra there are asters, larkspurs, mountain laurels, and fireweed, as well as mosses, lichens, and sedges. Wildflowers such as shooting stars, lupine, and anemones highlight vast stretches of Alaska's landscape with their brilliant colors.

Black bears, brown bears, grizzly bears, and polar bears are all native to Alaska. A large colony of Kodiak (Alaskan brown) bears inhabit Kodiak Island. This species is the largest carnivorous land mammal in the world. Herds of caribou roam the Arctic Slope and the Brooks Range, while shaggy musk-oxen thrive on Nunivak Island. Mountain goats and long-haired Dall sheep are found in many of the mountain ranges. Other animals found in Alaska include moose, elk, reindeer, wolves, beavers, foxes, muskrats, and raccoons.

Strict conservation laws protect Alaska's marine mammals. These include walruses, porpoises, sea otters, seals, sea lions, and whales. However, native peoples who traditionally hunt these animals for subsistence—that is, to provide for their basic needs—are exempted from these laws. The furry sea otter, which paddles through the water on its back, was once almost extinct from overhunting. The largest fur-seal herd in the world gathers on the Pribilof Islands. During the summer mating season, more than one million seals congregate on the island's beaches.

Alaska's native sea and shore birds include ducks, geese, swans, cranes, loons, gulls, petrels, puffins, plovers, and snipes. On the shores of Bristol Bay, the feathers of molting seabirds sometimes pile up as deep as 18 inches (46 centimeters). Bald and golden eagles, peregrine falcons, ravens, magpies, and jays are found throughout much of the state. Chilkat Bald Eagle Preserve near Haines hosts the largest gathering of bald eagles in the world.

Salmon, herring, cod, and halibut are important commercial fish. Trout, grayling, northern pike, Arctic char, and whitefish are mainly game fish. Amphibians that can weather Alaska's climate include a few species of salamanders, frogs, and toads. However, there are virtually no reptiles in Alaska.

## CLIMATE

Ocean currents, mountain ranges, winds, and frigid waters make Alaska a land of many climates. Southern and southeastern

The Matanuska Valley, in south-central Alaska, is known for its rich farmland.

Alaska enjoy a milder climate than the rest of the state. Here, temperatures are moderated by warm winds blowing in from the Pacific Ocean's Japan Current. On the southern coast, the average January temperature is about 28 degrees Fahrenheit (minus 2 degrees Celsius), and the July average is about 55 degrees Fahrenheit (13 degrees Celsius).

Without the benefit of ocean breezes, Alaska's interior is colder in the winter and warmer in the summer than land along the coasts. Thus, January's average temperature drops to about minus 9 degrees Fahrenheit (minus 23 degrees Celsius), while July averages about 59 degrees Fahrenheit (15 degrees Celsius). In fact, Alaska's interior has experienced both the record high and the record low temperatures in the state. On June 27, 1915, Fort Yukon set the record high at 100 degrees Fahrenheit (38 degrees Celsius). Prospect Creek set the record low on January 23, 1971, registering minus 80 degrees Fahrenheit (minus 62 degrees Celsius).

The Arctic region is not as bitterly cold as one might imagine. Here, as in the south, ocean waters moderate the air temperature and prevent the extreme cold found in the interior. Arctic Alaska averages minus 11 degrees Fahrenheit (minus 24 degrees Celsius) in January and 47 degrees Fahrenheit (8 degrees Celsius) in July.

Precipitation (moisture such as rain and snow) also varies from one region to another. The wettest region is the southeast, where some areas may receive more than 200 inches (508 centimeters) of precipitation a year. The average annual precipitation at Port Walter, on Baranof Island, is 221 inches (561 centimeters) — the highest recorded in the continental United States.

## THE NORTHERN LIGHTS

Serpents, drapes, and whirlpools of light in crimsons, purples, and greens — these are some of the ways people have described the aurora borealis, or northern lights. Filling the night sky with spectacular colors, the auroral displays appear over the Arctic Circle, most frequently occurring in spring and fall. A similar display, called the aurora australis, can be seen over Antarctica, on the opposite end of the earth.

Early native peoples believed the aurora to be ghostly fires or spirits of the dead. By now, however, scientists have determined that the phenomenon is caused by energized electrons striking gas molecules in the earth's upper atmosphere. Variations in color depend on how hard the electrons strike the gas particles.

## THE MIDNIGHT SUN

One of Alaska's many nicknames is Land of the Midnight Sun. But does the sun really shine at midnight there? The answer is yes, and some simple astronomy can explain why.

As the North Pole tilts toward the sun, summertime arrives in the Northern Hemisphere, and the days grow longer. The closer

**The beauty and splendor of the northern lights (left) and the soft glow of the midnight sun (right) fascinate Alaskans and visitors alike.**

the North Pole leans toward the sun, the more daylight hours there are in a summer's day. On June 20 or 21, called the summer solstice, the North Pole is closest to the sun, and the daylight period is at its peak.

The Arctic Circle is the latitude at which the summer solstice is twenty-four hours long! At that latitude around the globe, the sun never sets for one whole day. The farther north one goes, the longer that "longest day" is. With more than one-fourth of the state lying north of the Arctic Circle, it is easy to see why Alaska is called the Land of the Midnight Sun.

Barrow, the Alaskan city nearest to the North Pole, experiences the most drastic daylight extremes. After the sun rises over Barrow on May 10, it does not set again until August 2. That amounts to eighty-four days of continuous daylight! In the winter, after the sun sets on November 18, there is no more daylight in Barrow for sixty-seven days. The sun finally rises again on January 24.

# Chapter 3
# THE PEOPLE

# THE PEOPLE

## POPULATION AND POPULATION DISTRIBUTION

In terms of population, Alaska ranks next-to-last among the fifty states. Only Wyoming has fewer residents. The 1980 census listed Alaska's population as 401,851. However, Alaska is one of the fastest-growing states in the country. During the 1970s, the state's population increased by a surprising 33 percent. The United States Census Bureau estimated that, by 1985, Alaska's population had increased to 521,000.

With their small population spread out over the largest land area of all the states, Alaskans enjoy plenty of living space. There are an average of 68 Alaskans per 100 square miles (26 per 100 square kilometers). In the United States as a whole, the population is close to one hundred times as dense. The national average is 67 people per square mile (26 people per square kilometer).

About 64 percent of Alaskans live in urban areas. More than 40 percent of the state's residents—174,431 people—live in Anchorage, the largest city. Fairbanks (22,645 people) and Juneau, the state capital (19,528 people), are the other major centers of population.

The majority of Alaska's vast land area, however, is sparsely populated. Dozens of Alaskan towns—such as Chicken, with a population of thirty-seven—have fewer than one hundred residents.

# WHO ARE THE ALASKANS?

About two-thirds of all Alaskans were born outside the state. Many of these transplanted residents are oil-industry workers, military personnel, or other government workers. Native-born Alaskans include both native peoples and the descendants of early settlers.

In the early 1900s, many miners, fishermen, and lumber workers moved in from the western states. Others came from Canada, Scandinavia, the Balkans, Japan, and the Philippines. Alaska, rich in natural resources, offered them promising work opportunities. The Great Depression of the 1930s brought more new arrivals looking for better farming and living conditions.

During World War II (1939-45), several thousand military construction engineers and civilian laborers were sent to Alaska to build highways and military facilities. Many of these workers returned after the war to pursue Alaskan lifestyles and job opportunities. Military construction projects in the early 1950s brought another wave of newcomers into Alaska. In the 1970s, laborers poured into the state once again, this time to help construct the Trans-Alaska Pipeline.

Only 3 percent of Alaska's people are black, though their numbers are gradually increasing. Most live and work in the Anchorage area. Hispanics comprise less than 2 percent of the population. Dozens of other ethnic groups contribute to Alaska's cultural diversity. Many have come across the Pacific Ocean from Japan, South Korea, Taiwan, the Philippines, and other Asian countries. Alaska's strong antidiscrimination measures have benefited all the state's ethnic groups, although these laws were primarily designed to help Alaska's native peoples.

Among Alaska's native peoples are the Inupiat Eskimos of Kotzebue (left) and the Tlingit Indians of Kake, a village on Kupreanof Island (right).

## NATIVE PEOPLES

Alaska's native peoples make up about 16 percent of the population. There are three major groups of Alaskan natives: the Eskimos, the Aleuts, and the Indians.

More than half of Alaska's natives are Eskimos. According to various estimates, they number from thirty-four thousand to forty-two thousand. Living largely by their expert hunting and fishing skills, the Eskimos occupy the islands and coastlands along the Arctic Ocean and the Bering Sea. Some Eskimos also dwell in the Yukon and Kuskokwim river valleys, on Kodiak Island, on the southern coast of the Kenai Peninsula, and on the Alaska Peninsula.

There are two major groups of Eskimos. The Inupiat Eskimos live in the north and northwest. From the Arctic Ocean they spread inland to the Brooks Range, where Anaktuvuk Pass is an important Inupiat village. The Eskimos in western Alaska, along the Bering Sea, are the Yupik Eskimos.

The smallest group of Alaskan natives, the Aleuts, live on the Aleutian Islands and the Alaska Peninsula. There are also Aleut settlements on the Pribilof Islands of Saint Paul and Saint George. Today, the Aleut population numbers about eight thousand.

About twenty-four thousand Alaskan natives are Indians. They are divided into two groups: the interior Indians and the maritime Indians. The Athabascan Indians occupy Alaska's great interior and include several subgroups of peoples. On the islands and in the forests of the southeast live Alaska's three groups of maritime Indians—the Tlingits, the Haidas, and the Tsimshians.

Today, about ten thousand Tlingit people occupy Alaska's Panhandle. Major Haida population centers are the towns of Hydaburg and Kasaan in the Prince of Wales Archipelago. The Haidas number between seven hundred and eight hundred today. About one thousand Tsimshians live at Metlakatla on Annette Island, the only Tsimshian settlement in the state.

## ALASKAN LIFESTYLES

In Alaska's largest cities and towns, people live much like their neighbors in the Lower 48. Office buildings mark the skylines of cities such as Anchorage and Fairbanks, and people commute to their offices by car or public transportation from houses, condominiums, or apartments.

Juneau, Alaska's capital and third-largest city, can be reached only by water or air. No practical roads cross the Coast Mountains that rise behind Juneau to the east. Nor do roads connect Juneau with other cities along the Panhandle or with the islands of the Alexander Archipelago.

In Alaska's rugged, sparsely populated regions, known as the bush, people live quite differently than city dwellers. In many remote areas, there are no roads, and people fly in and out in bush planes. During the long winter season, when daylight hours are short and heavy snows confine people to their homes, residents of the bush can suffer "cabin fever." Although the term is often used jokingly, the symptoms—loneliness, isolation, and depression—are real.

Those who live in the Arctic region face special problems. Among them is permafrost, the Arctic's frozen subsoil. When a house is built on permafrost, heat from inside the house can thaw the permafrost beneath it. The thawed soil begins to sink down, and the house tilts or sags. Some Arctic dwellers build their houses on skids, or wooden platforms, so they can be moved from time to time. A homeowner in Nome claimed to have moved his house seven times!

For oil-industry workers around Prudhoe Bay, life is rather bleak. Employees work twelve hours a day, seven days a week. Most live in group housing centers. There is no outside entertainment and nowhere to go. Every few weeks, the employees get a week or two of vacation and fly out to their own homes.

Some of Alaska's native peoples still carry on a subsistence lifestyle. For many Eskimos, survival depends on hunting and processing whales, walruses, and seals. The meat, hides, and fat of these animals provide the Eskimos with food, clothing, heating fuel, tools, and even some home-building materials. Some Aleuts continue to build barabaras, which are sod houses supported by whalebone or driftwood. Other native peoples, however, have moved to the cities and adapted to nonnative jobs or lifestyles. Still others combine old ways and new. The Inupiat Eskimos of Point Hope, for instance, still use umiaks—open, wood-frame boats covered with hides—to hunt whales. At the same time, they use walkie-talkies and modern whaling guns. Many Aleuts earn a living as seal hunters or commercial fishermen, and some maritime Indians work in the fishing, logging, lumbering, and pulp industries.

## RELIGION

All the major religions practiced in the Lower 48 are represented in Alaska. The Roman Catholic church, with more than forty-six thousand members, is the largest religious group. Large Protestant denominations, whose missionaries began preaching in Alaska in the 1800s, include Presbyterian, Episcopalian, Lutheran, Baptist, and Methodist. Houses of worship for members of the Jewish, Baha'i, Christian Science, Assemblies of God, Church of God, Alaskan Moravian, and Mormon faiths are also found in Alaska. The Russian Orthodox church has many native members throughout Alaska, especially in the Aleutian Islands and the southeast.

## POLITICS

Except for the year 1964, when their electoral votes went to Democrat Lyndon B. Johnson, Alaskans supported the Republican presidential candidate in every election year since statehood. State and local voting patterns have leaned toward the Democrats, however. When Alaskans went to the polls in November 1958 to choose their first state officials, they elected Democrats to the governorship and to the United States Congress. Only two Republicans have won the governor's race since then. It was not until 1966 that Alaskans first sent a Republican to Congress.

Still, party politics is not a significant factor for Alaska's voters. Most state and local officeholders are appointed to their posts, and many elected officials run as nonpartisan candidates.

# Chapter 4
# THE BEGINNING

# THE BEGINNING

## PREHISTORIC ALASKA

About eighteen thousand years ago, at the peak of the earth's great Ice Age, much of the earth's water was in the form of ice. Great masses of land now covered with water were dry. One of these land masses stretched between what are now northeastern Siberia and Alaska. Called Beringia, or the Bering Land Bridge, this great low-lying plain now lies beneath the Bering and Chukchi seas.

Prehistoric animals, most of them extinct today, migrated across Beringia and roamed Alaska's grasslands. Paleontologists and archaeologists have learned about these animals from fossil remains—and from discovering entire animals frozen in ice, almost perfectly preserved.

Prehistoric Alaska's animals included woolly mammoths, steppe bisons, miniature horses, mastodons, antelopes, musk-oxen, moose, camels, sloths, lions, and saber-toothed tigers. People called Paleo-Indians hunted many of these beasts with weapons they made from chipped stone.

## THE FIRST ALASKANS

Archaeologists believe that the ancestors of today's native Alaskans also crossed Beringia from Siberia, beginning perhaps as early as fifteen thousand years ago. Though the Bering Land Bridge was covered by water about fourteen thousand years ago,

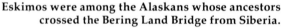
Eskimos were among the Alaskans whose ancestors crossed the Bering Land Bridge from Siberia.

crossings continued by boat. In waves of migration spanning several thousand years, bands of nomads spread northeast in search of fish, game, and edible plants. These early Alaskans eventually formed three distinct groups: Eskimos, Aleuts, and Indians.

The Eskimos, who inhabited northern and western Alaska, were great hunters. Across the northern tundra, they stalked herds of caribou and musk-oxen for their meat and hides. They also hunted walruses, seals, polar bears, and birds. In skin-covered boats called kayaks, the Eskimos harpooned massive whales. The whale fat, or blubber, provided cooking and heating fuel.

The seafaring Aleuts occupied southwest Alaska, or what is now the Aleutian Islands. The flesh, hides, and bones of shore and sea animals provided the Aleuts with food, clothing, shelter, heating materials, and tools. In baidarkas, the Aleuts' skin-covered canoes, they ventured hundreds of miles out from their homes.

**Ancestors of these Athabascan Indians occupied prehistoric Alaska.**

The Aleut word *al-ay-es-ka*, meaning "great land," eventually
gave Alaska its name.

Two great Indian nations occupied prehistoric Alaska as well:
the Athabascans and the Tlingits. Relatives of the Navaho and
Apache Indians of the southwestern United States, the
Athabascans settled in Alaska's vast interior. Skilled hunters, they
tracked moose and caribou through the central forests and plains.
The Athabascans developed snowshoes for walking on top of the
snow as they hunted. They fished the rivers for salmon and traded
furs and other goods with the Eskimos and Tlingits. Competition
for hunting and fishing grounds often resulted in conflicts
between Athabascans and Eskimos.

The Tlingits occupied the forests and coastlands of Alaska's
southeast. Blessed with a mild climate, they thrived on the
plentiful fish, game, and edible plants of the southeast. They also
enjoyed a highly developed cultural and artistic life. On

elaborately carved totem poles, they recorded their ancient stories, legends, and family histories. Superb artisans, they fashioned intricate ceremonial garments and exquisite blankets.

## THE HAIDAS

Moving into Tlingit territory from Canada in the early 1700s, the Haidas settled in the Prince of Wales Archipelago at the southern end of Alaska's Panhandle. Like the Tlingits, the Haidas recorded information by carving totem poles. They also developed precise and delicate artistry using bones and shells.

Living in the southeast's rich forestlands, the Tlingits and Haidas were also expert woodworkers. They hollowed out dugout canoes and built well-constructed clan houses. They also made bentwood boxes, dugout bowls, and spruce-root baskets.

## BERING'S FIRST VOYAGE

In the 1700s, Russian czar Peter the Great began to turn his attention to the lands east of Siberia. Siberia was the desolate region on the eastern edge of the great Russian empire.

Peter, ruler of Russia from 1689 to 1725, enthusiastically supported the sciences. He listened intently as mapmakers debated whether America and Asia were joined at their northern reaches. In 1724, Peter appointed Vitus Bering, a Dane serving in the Russian navy, to head a full-scale expedition to the Kamchatka Peninsula on Siberia's eastern coast. From there, Bering was to make a voyage to find out whether Asia and America were connected by land.

Bering was a faithful officer but had little scientific curiosity. He carried out his mission, but more with an attitude of duty than of exploration. For a year and a half, Bering cut across thousands of miles of Siberia's frigid forests and jagged mountain ranges. By 1727, he and a crew of shipbuilders and sailors had reached Okhotsk, in southern Siberia. There he built a ship, the *Saint Gabriel*, and launched it in July 1728.

Sailing north, Bering and his crew reached an island, which he named Saint Lawrence Island, in what is now called the Bering Sea. Continuing north, they passed through the narrow waters between Siberia's Chukotsk (Chukchi) Peninsula and Alaska's Seward Peninsula. That channel, now called the Bering Strait, was so clouded with fog and rain that Bering saw nothing as he looked to the east. Nor did he search for American shores, though he surely knew they lay nearby. Instead, Bering returned to Russia and filed his report. The two continents were not joined, he said, but he had not sighted America.

## THE SECOND EXPEDITION

In the spring of 1741, Bering went on a second expedition, this time with Russian explorer Aleksey Chirikov. Their assignment was to find America. Plagued by constant rain and fog, changing currents, and shifting winds, Bering was no more enthusiastic about this mission than he had been about the one before. His ship, the *Saint Peter*, and Chirikov's, the *Saint Paul*, became separated during the voyage, never to be rejoined.

The two ships spent weeks wandering in the foggy seas. On July 15, Chirikov spotted land at the southern end of Alaska's Panhandle and sent two boatloads of men toward shore. Had they landed, they would have been the first Europeans on Alaskan soil. This will never be known, however, for the men were never seen again. Five months later, Chirikov returned to Kamchatka.

After Vitus Bering's crew returned to Russia with a cargo of fur pelts, Russian merchants immediately began sending expeditions to Alaska for the prized pelts of sea otters, seals (right), and other fur-bearing animals.

On July 16, the clouds parted over Bering's crew, and before them rose the Saint Elias mountain range, near Alaska's southern coast. They dropped anchor on what is now Kayak Island and went ashore, thus becoming the first Europeans known to set foot on Alaskan land.

On the return trip, many of Bering's crew members weakened or died from scurvy, a disease caused by a lack of vitamin C. Violent storms forced the captain to harbor the *Saint Peter* on an island off the Kamchatka Peninsula. There the ship was wrecked and, in December 1742, Bering died. That island was named Bering Island in his honor.

Surviving members of Bering's crew managed to rebuild the *Saint Peter* and return to Russia with news of their landing on American soil. It was their cargo, however, that drew the most attention. From Alaska's islands and coastlands, they brought hundreds of fur pelts from animals they had hunted or trapped. The most prized of them all was the luxurious skin of the sea otter.

Instantly, Russia's interest in Alaska focused on its furs. In the great market of Canton, Chinese traders were willing to pay enormous sums for sea-otter pelts. Russian merchants began sending expeditions to Alaska's Aleutian Islands and Kodiak Island for sea otters, as well as blue foxes, seals, and other fur-bearing animals.

## COLONIZATION AND EXPLORATION

By 1745, Russian merchant crews were actively trading for furs on Alaska's westernmost islands. They took command wherever they landed, forcing the inhabitants to work for them and pay taxes in furs. Aleuts—natives of the Aleutian Islands and expert hunters—were used as slaves and were forced to hunt for the fur traders. The Russians almost exterminated the Aleut population of twenty-five thousand. By the end of the 1700s, only two thousand Aleuts remained.

As word of the new land spread, British, Spanish, and French explorers soon plied Alaska's waters. Some searched for a trade route to Asia, while others hoped to establish colonies.

From Spain's colony of Mexico, Spanish captains sailed up America's western coast, claiming land as they went along. In 1773, Juan Perez reached the southern coast of Alaska in his ship the *Santiago*. Spanish captain Juan Francisco de la Bodega y Quadra, sailing in the *Sonora*, landed near Sitka in 1775 and claimed Alaska's southern coast for Spain. Four years later, a third Spanish expedition sailed as far as present-day Cook Inlet. Alaskan towns such as Valdez and Cordova trace their names to the time of these Spanish explorations.

In 1776, two British captains, James Cook and Charles Clerke, set out to find a route from the Atlantic Ocean to the Pacific. Reaching Alaskan waters in 1778, Cook sailed as far north as the Bering Strait. Captain Clerke continued north as far as Point Lay.

During the voyage of Captain James Cook (right) in 1778, one of the expedition's artists made an engraving of Unalaska's Aleuts and their kayaks (above).

In 1786, French captain Jean François Galaup, Count Pérouse, sailed near land in the northern region of southeastern Alaska. He sighted Mount Saint Elias and spent three months trading with and studying the Tlingit Indians.

In 1792, one of James Cook's lieutenants, Captain George Vancouver, returned to Alaska. For two years he explored, surveyed, and accurately charted Alaska's Pacific Coast up to Cook Inlet. He gave British names to such places as Prince William Sound, Cape Prince of Wales, and Bristol Bay. Vancouver's charts remained useful geographical surveys of the area for the next hundred years.

## REIGN OF THE TRADING COMPANIES

By the late 1700s, Russia had granted charters to two great trading companies for the fur trade in Russian America, as Alaska was now called. The Lebedev-Lastochkin Company was allowed to hunt and trap in Cook Inlet and the Pribilof Islands. The

**Sitka, renamed New Archangel, was the official headquarters for the Russian-American Company.**

Shelikhov-Golikov Company was to have Kodiak Island. There, in 1784, Grigory Shelikhov established the Russians' first permanent settlement at Three Saints Bay.

In 1799, the Russian-American Company, which grew from the Shelikhov-Golikov Company, was chartered. Its manager, Aleksandr Baranov, established a settlement near present-day Sitka on Alaska's southeast coast. Native Tlingits, who had lived in the area for hundreds of years, resented the invasion not only of Russian traders but also of the British and Americans. In 1802, the Tlingits attacked the Russian settlement, killing most of the Russians and their Aleut slaves.

Two years later, Baranov returned with Russian troops and Aleuts to wreak revenge upon the Tlingits. For six days, the Tlingits bravely stood their ground. Finally, having run out of ammunition, the Indians abandoned their fortifications in the middle of the night.

Baranov rebuilt his settlement, naming it New Archangel. Soon the town became the official headquarters for the Russian-

American Company and an important center for foreign trade. While some residents, such as Baranov and the Russian Orthodox bishop, lived in elegant homes, most lived quite humbly. As Sir George Simpson of the Hudson's Bay Company wrote, "Of all the dirty and wretched places that I have ever seen, Sitka [its later name] is pre-eminently the most wretched and most dirty."

After Baranov retired in 1817, various Russian naval officers ran the Russian-American Company. Acting also as governors for Russian America, these officers trained and employed hundreds of natives and people of mixed European and native blood. Many worked on shipbuilding and other construction projects. Others were sent on expeditions up the Yukon and Kuskokwim rivers to establish posts and find new sources of furs.

Meanwhile, foreign fur traders, especially British and Americans, had been moving into the territory. Among the newcomers, England's Hudson's Bay Company was one of the most aggressive. Russian America's ruling officers decided to put a stop to these intrusions. In 1821, they acquired from the Russian government a *ukase*, or proclamation, prohibiting foreign traders in Alaska.

England and the United States loudly protested the ban. After negotiations among the three governments, Russia signed treaties with the United States in 1824 and Britain in 1825. These agreements granted the two countries limited trading privileges along the Pacific Coast and in the interior. The 54° 40' latitude— at the southern tip of Alaska's Panhandle—was also set as the southern boundary of Russian America.

These treaties did not settle trading conflicts, however. In 1834, at present-day Wrangell, Russian warships blocked a Hudson's Bay Company expedition that was headed up the Stikine River to establish a trading post. Traders from the United States were

**Cartoonists of the time jeered at Seward's purchase of a "chunk of ice" for $7.2 million.**

banned in 1835, but their whaling expeditions continued to hunt
in Alaskan waters.

The Russian-American Company's charter was renewed in
1841. Yet Russia, preoccupied with European wars, was growing
weary of its faraway colony. Interested only in furs, the company
was doing little to build up the colony and develop its agriculture,
fisheries, and mines. But the sea-otter population was dwindling,
and even fur seals were becoming hard to find. The cost of
supporting the colony was greater than the value of the furs
brought in. When the company's charter expired in 1861, Russia
did not renew it.

## THE PURCHASE OF SEWARD'S FOLLY

By this time, Russia knew that the United States was interested
in buying Alaska. Fishermen along North America's northwest
coast wanted the cod that abounded in Alaskan waters. Mining
companies in the United States had their eyes on Alaska's copper,
coal, and gold.

On March 30, 1867, the Treaty of Cession of Russian America to the United States was signed by Seward (holding pen) and Stoeckl (with hand on globe).

In 1859, California senator William McKendree Gwin had approached Edouard de Stoeckl, the Russian minister to the United States, with an unofficial offer of $5 million for the territory. While Russia considered the offer, the United States' attention turned to its own Civil War (1861-65). As a gesture of friendship, Russia sent a fleet of ships to the United States to support the Union side.

Once the war was over, United States secretary of state William H. Seward began serious negotiations for the purchase of Alaska. Many people in the United States, believing Alaska to be a frozen wasteland, thought this was a foolish idea. Newspapers jeered, calling the territory "Seward's Folly" and "Seward's Icebox." Some called it "Walrussia," referring to the territory's walruses.

Even foreigners scoffed at Seward's attraction to Alaska. "Mr. Seward's mania for icebergs and snow-fields," wrote Englishman Frederick Whymper, "seems insatiable."

On October 18, 1867, at a ceremony in Sitka, the Russian flag was lowered and the American flag was raised, formally transferring ownership of Russian America to the United States.

Nevertheless, Seward persisted and, on March 29, 1867, Russia agreed to sell. Next, the United States Senate had to approve the sale, but the senators were due to adjourn the next day. On the night of March 29, Stoeckl showed up at Seward's home. The two agreed to meet at the State Department at midnight, and by 4:00 A.M. on March 30, the treaty of sale was completed and signed. The final price was set at $7.2 million—less than two cents per acre (five cents per hectare). By 10:00 A.M., Seward had the treaty before the senators, who remained in session until they approved the sale on April 9.

On October 18, 1867, at a ceremony in Sitka, Russia formally transferred ownership of Russian America to the United States. At the ceremony, wrote Whymper, "The Russian flag showed great reluctance to come down, and stuck on the yard-arm of the flag-staff. A man was sent up to detach the halyards, when it fell on the heads of the Russian soldiers appointed its defenders."

Overcome with embarrassment, the Russian governor's wife burst into tears, but the program went on. The American flag was raised, twenty-one guns fired a salute, and three cheers rose up from the crowd. Russian America was now United States soil.

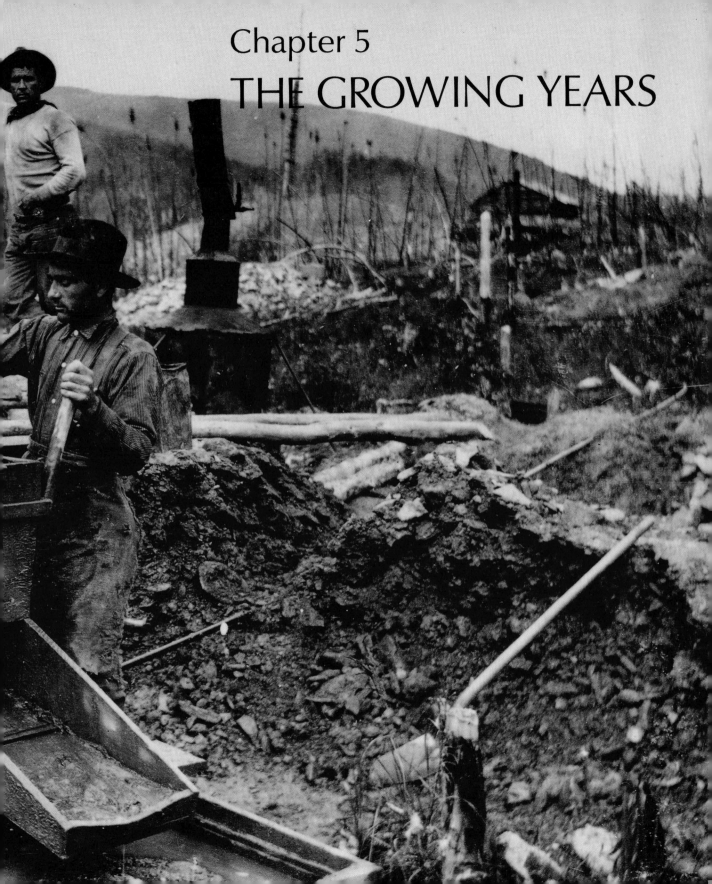

Chapter 5
# THE GROWING YEARS

# THE GROWING YEARS

For all the furor that surrounded the Alaska purchase, the United States seemed to have tucked the territory away after the sale and forgotten about it. For the next ten years, the United States War Department was in charge of Alaskan affairs. This ended in 1877, when army troops in Alaska were summoned to Idaho to help fight the Nez Perce Indians.

Only United States customs officials remained to govern this vast, sprawling land. In 1879, the USS *Jamestown* arrived, and for the next five years the United States Navy governed Alaska's affairs.

On May 17, 1884, Congress passed an Organic Act creating the District of Alaska, and John H. Kinkead was appointed governor. The act provided a civil government by extending the laws of Oregon to Alaska.

In 1887, a new group of Indians—the Tsimshians—arrived in southeastern Alaska from British Columbia, led by Anglican missionary William Duncan.

## THE GOLD RUSH

Ever since gold had been discovered in California in 1848, prospectors had been combing the West Coast looking for more. From time to time, rumors of Alaskan gold trickled down to the Lower 48. In 1867, a San Francisco newspaper reported that native women in Alaska "wear necklaces of gold and nuggets picked up from the surface."

**The discovery of gold near present-day Juneau resulted in the creation of a thriving boomtown.**

Only scant traces of the metal had turned up in Alaska, though, until Joe Juneau and Dick Harris made their big strike near the present-day city of Juneau. While probing the southeastern waterways in 1880, their Tlingit guides led them to rich gold deposits along the Gastineau Channel. Soon droves of prospectors poured into the region, set up tents, and scurried about the hills and streams with picks and pans. The "tent cities" of Juneau, Douglas, and Treadwell grew into boomtowns, and Juneau's mines were active for decades.

From there, prospectors penetrated deep into Alaska's interior. Deposits were found at Forty Mile in 1886 and Birch Creek in 1892. Each new discovery drew hundreds of fortune hunters.

Still, the biggest strike of them all was yet to come. Discovery of gold in the Klondike region of Canada's Yukon Territory in 1896

The Klondike gold rush brought thousands of prospectors to Skagway.

touched off a fevered rush for gold. Stampedes of prospectors swelled Alaskan towns on their way to the Yukon. The population of Skagway, a major entry point to the Klondike, soared to twenty thousand. The town, wrote naturalist John Muir, was like "a nest of ants taken into a strange country and stirred up by a stick."

More gold rushers swarmed to the beaches of Nome on the Seward Peninsula after gold was discovered there in 1899. The town of Fairbanks grew up after Felix Pedro's gold strike there in 1902. Between 1890 and 1900, Alaska's population almost doubled because of the gold fever.

## TERRITORIAL DAYS

Slowly, Alaska began to catch the federal government's attention. In 1900, Alaska was given its own code of laws and Juneau was made the capital.

**Alaska's new territorial legislature met for the first time on March 3, 1913.**

In 1906, Alaskans were finally allowed to elect a delegate to the United States House of Representatives, although he would not be allowed to vote. Democrat Frank H. Waskey was Alaska's first delegate to Congress. Judge James Wickersham, a later delegate who was first seated in 1909, worked long and hard in Washington to further Alaskans' interests.

In 1912, Congress passed the Second Organic Act for Alaska, granting it official status as a United States territory. The following year, on March 3, 1913, Alaska's new territorial legislature met for its first session. Among its first acts, the legislature approved voting rights for Alaskan women. It was not until 1920 that the Nineteenth Amendment to the United States Constitution gave all the nation's women the right to vote.

Already, many Alaskans were beginning to hope for statehood. They felt that Alaskan affairs would be managed better from home than from Washington, D.C.

**The government experimental farm in the Matanuska Valley**

Dozens of new towns had sprung up during the gold rush, and they were still growing. But gold had turned out to be just one of Alaska's many natural treasures. Coal had been discovered at Cook Inlet, and the Kennecott copper mines were flourishing north of Cordova. Alaska's rich salmon fisheries were supporting busy canneries in the southeast.

Congressman Wickersham introduced an Alaska statehood bill in Congress in 1916, but it did not pass. In 1917, when the United States entered World War I (1914-18), Alaska's population dropped as many residents entered the military. This made it more difficult for the territory to meet the population requirements for statehood.

The territory's population once again increased, however, when the Great Depression of the 1930s brought many Americans from the Lower 48 to Alaska. To help them start a new life, the federal government resettled two hundred farm families from the midwestern United States in Alaska's fertile Matanuska Valley.

On May 11, 1943, American troops landed on the Japanese-held island of Attu.

## WORLD WAR II

After Japan bombed the United States military base at Pearl Harbor, Hawaii, in December 1941, the United States entered World War II. A flood of military personnel and civilian workers soon poured into Alaska. To provide a land route for military equipment, the United States government brought thousands of workers into Alaska and Canada to build what is now called the Alaska Highway. Under the direction of the United States Army Corps of Engineers, the Alaska-Canada Military Highway (or Alcan) was completed in only eight months. Before long, the United States troop count in Alaska had risen to about 152,000 people.

There was a reason for this spirit of urgency: Alaska's westernmost islands lay dangerously close to Japan. The United States' concern was justified. On June 3, 1942, Japanese bombers struck the United States Navy base at Dutch Harbor in the

Aleutian Islands. Four days later, Japanese combat troops invaded the islands of Attu and Kiska, the only North American soil to be occupied during the war.

In May 1943, American forces fought furiously to reclaim Attu. United States casualties in this conflict were high. Considering the number of troops engaged in the Battle of Attu, the proportion of casualties was second only to those suffered at Iwo Jima. By the end of August 1943, Kiska was also back in American hands.

## STATEHOOD AT LAST

After the war ended in 1945, many military and civilian workers returned to Alaska to live. In time, the outcry for statehood swelled, the loudest cries coming from Anchorage and Fairbanks. Alaskans were becoming more and more annoyed with their status as "second-class citizens." For example, they could not vote in presidential elections, and their governors were appointed without their vote.

To prove they were ready for statehood, Alaskans decided to draw up a state constitution. In 1955, they elected fifty-five delegates from all over the territory to meet in Fairbanks for a constitutional convention. For seventy-three days the delegates labored, eventually producing a document that has been called "one of the best, if not the best, state constitutions ever written." Alaskans voted their approval of the constitution in 1956.

Finally, on May 28, 1958, the United States House of Representatives approved a statehood enabling act for Alaska. The Senate approved the act on June 30. On July 7, 1958, President Dwight D. Eisenhower signed the act into law.

Alaskans went to the polls on August 26 to voice their wishes and, by a resounding margin of five to one, voted in favor of

In July 1959, this bell outside the Federal Building was rung forty-nine times, in honor of Alaska's joining the Union as the forty-ninth state.

statehood. On January 3, 1959, President Eisenhower officially declared Alaska the forty-ninth state in the Union.

On July 4, at a ceremony in Juneau, the new United States flag—now with forty-nine stars—was officially raised. Next was hoisted Alaska's old territorial flag, now the official state flag. The banner was familiar to all the crowd: eight gold stars—the Big Dipper and the North Star—on a field of blue. Among the onlookers was Benny Benson, his head held high. As a thirteen-year-old in 1926, Benny had designed Alaska's flag. At the time, he had written these prophetic words: "The North Star is for the future state of Alaska, the most northerly of the Union." Benny had waited thirty-three years to see his vision come true.

Chapter 6
ON TO THE TWENTY-
FIRST CENTURY

# ON TO THE TWENTY-FIRST CENTURY

Alaskans took to their long-awaited statehood with vigor and pride. They elected Democrat William A. Egan as their first state governor. Old territorial departments became state departments and, in accordance with the new state constitution, the governor appointed the department heads. Now, too, Alaskans could send a voting representative and two senators to the United States Congress.

Tragically, two serious disasters in the 1960s dampened the state's spirits. On Good Friday—March 27, 1964—the Anchorage area was devastated by the strongest earthquake ever to hit the North American continent. Initially registering between 8.4 and 8.6 on the Richter scale, the quake's magnitude was later revised to 9.2. The Good Friday earthquake, with its accompanying seismic wave, caused the death or disappearance of more than one hundred people and property damage of some $400 million. Then in 1967, Fairbanks suffered the worst flood in its history. Five persons died in the flood, and damages rose to over $84 million.

## OIL!

Since 1957, a commercial well had been pumping oil on the Kenai Peninsula. Alaska's most spectacular oil strike came in

The March 27, 1964, earthquake caused the collapse of this street in Anchorage.

1968, however, when large oil reserves were discovered at Prudhoe Bay on Alaska's Arctic Slope. The following year, Alaska began auctioning oil and gas leases on the Prudhoe Bay oil field. A major problem for the oil extracting companies, however, was how to get the oil to market. Shipping it all the way around Alaska in oil tankers seemed out of the question. An oil pipeline straight through Alaska's interior seemed to them the best solution.

The pipeline proposal soon sparked a passionate campaign by both local and out-of-state environmentalists. A major leakage or spill, they felt, could seriously endanger the state's wildlife and wilderness areas.

As battles raged in conference rooms and in the local and national press, resident Alaskans chose sides, too. Vehicle bumper stickers throughout the state blared owners' sentiments in pointed prose. Residents of Cordova filed a lawsuit to prevent the pipeline's terminal from being located in nearby Valdez. The Cordovans' entire economy depended on fishing, and an oil spill could wipe out their livelihood. Some of Alaska's natives protested, too, as the pipeline would cross their reserved lands. Finally, after specially designed safety features were included and native claims were settled, the pipeline was approved. Construction began in 1974.

Eight oil companies formed the Alyeska Pipeline Service Company to build and manage the pipeline. Costing a total of $8 billion, it would extend from Prudhoe Bay to the port of Valdez on the Gulf of Alaska. In 1977, the 800-mile (1,287-kilometer) Trans-Alaska Pipeline was completed, and oil production at Prudhoe Bay began.

The first "black gold" to course through the pipeline reached Valdez on July 28, 1977. As a tanker pulled away from port with the first shipment of oil, it carried a cargo worth $7.2 million— the same price the United States paid for all of Alaska in 1867!

## REVENUE REVOLUTION

Alaska's newborn oil industry took the state on an economic roller-coaster ride. Population and employment figures soared while pipeline construction was underway. When construction was completed, the state's economy fell into a slump. By 1980, however, tremendous oil revenues were pouring into the state's treasury. Local and state governments rushed into a flurry of new construction, building community centers, schools, highways, airstrips, and remote satellite receiving stations.

Oil benefits to Alaskans went further still. In 1976, Alaskans approved an amendment to their constitution that created the

The Port of Anchorage is a busy cargo port and oil-storage facility.

Permanent Fund. The amendment set aside one-fourth of the state's oil and other mineral revenues to benefit Alaska's future generations. From this fund, an annual dividend was to be divided among Alaskans who had been residents for at least six months. The first checks were mailed in 1982. As of 1979, Alaska's legislature abolished the state personal income tax and provided for home-loan subsidies and a large student-loan fund.

Unfortunately, a drop in world oil prices in 1985 sent the state into a recession. So much of Alaska's economy was tied into the oil industry that economic activity declined statewide.

## ALASKA NATIVE CLAIMS SETTLEMENT ACT

While oil was revolutionizing the state's economy, Alaska's natives were going through a revolution of their own. In 1971, the United States Congress passed the Alaska Native Claims Settlement Act (ANCSA). In an effort to correct land-rights injustices, this act assigned 44 million acres (18 million hectares) of Alaskan land and $962.5 million to Alaska's Eskimos, Aleuts, and Indians. It was the largest settlement that the United States government had ever paid to any Native American peoples.

To manage these newly acquired assets, thirteen regional native business corporations and more than two hundred village corporations were formed. Native corporations now operate such businesses as seafood canneries, lumber and pulp mills, and mines. The ANCSA also provided that, beginning in 1991, native corporations could begin selling stock to nonnatives.

## LAND USE CONTROVERSIES

In 1980, Congress passed the Alaska National Interest Lands Conservation Act (ANILCA), usually referred to as the Alaska Lands Act. This measure added 104 million acres (42 million hectares) to Alaska's national parklands, more than doubling the state's federal lands. While environmentalists welcomed the Alaska Lands Act as a victory, not all Alaskans were as enthusiastic. After the act was passed, a full 60 percent of Alaskan land was controlled by the federal government.

Heated dispute in the late 1980s and early 1990s focused on the Arctic National Wildlife Refuge (ANWR). Large oil and gas deposits were believed to lie beneath the surface of this vast refuge. Oil producers, environmentalists, and the United States Congress hotly debated about the environmental effects of drilling for these resources, about native land ownership, and about other sensitive issues.

## EXXON VALDEZ OIL SPILL

In 1989, Alaska suffered yet another Good Friday disaster. Shortly after midnight on March 24, after leaving the port of

Valdez, the oil tanker *Exxon Valdez* struck a reef in Prince William Sound. Its hull gashed, the tanker spewed 11 million gallons (42 million liters) of crude oil into the sound. Due to high winds and shorthanded cleanup crews, the sticky black substance soon covered hundreds of miles of Alaska's southern coastline. Abounding with marine life, Prince William Sound suffered the loss of countless birds, fish, sea otters, and seals.

From all over the country, cleanup workers rushed to the site. Some extracted surface oil, while others scrubbed rocks or tried to salvage oil-coated fish and birds. Commercial fisheries along Prince William Sound closed, confirming the fears voiced by Cordova's residents nearly twenty years before.

The *Exxon Valdez* incident was the largest oil spill in United States history. It will probably take years to assess the spill's long-range effects on Alaska's environment and economy.

## A GLIMPSE INTO THE FUTURE

Alaskans look toward the twenty-first century with optimism. Although their cost of living is high, their per-capita income ranks among the highest in the country, and their economy is healthy enough to have weathered many setbacks. Income from tourism is on the rise, too, as cruise ships bring record numbers of sightseers into the state. The passage of the Magnuson Act of 1976, barring foreign fisheries from Alaska's 200-mile (322-kilometer) offshore Exclusive Economic Zone, has greatly boosted the state's seafood industry.

In the area of international relations, Alaska is also becoming increasingly important because of its position on the so-called Pacific Rim. Through closer diplomatic and economic ties, the United States is becoming more involved with the countries that

**Cleanup crews at work after the *Exxon Valdez* oil spill of March 24, 1989**

rim the Pacific Ocean. These include the Soviet Union, Japan, South Korea, Taiwan, the People's Republic of China, the Philippines, Indonesia, and Australia. As the state nearest to the Asian nations, Alaska has been a leader in communication, trade, and cultural exchange with these Pacific neighbors.

At the same time, Alaskans face some serious, ongoing concerns. Environmentalists, developers, and oil producers continue to battle over land-use issues. Nonresident workers are another continuous problem. Taking advantage of temporary work in Alaska, they take jobs away from Alaska's residents and then leave the state with their earnings.

Though natives stand to gain even more economic power in the future, many remain unskilled, poorly educated, and unemployed. Rooted in a subsistence lifestyle, but surrounded by Western ways, they find themselves citizens of two worlds. Bridging that gap remains their most urgent challenge.

# Chapter 7
# GOVERNMENT AND THE ECONOMY

# GOVERNMENT AND THE ECONOMY

## STATE GOVERNMENT

Like the federal government, Alaska's state government is divided into three branches. The legislative branch passes state laws. The executive branch, or office of the governor, sees that laws are carried out. The judicial branch, consisting of the state courts, interprets the laws.

Alaska's legislature consists of two houses: a twenty-member senate and a forty-member house of representatives. State senators are elected to four-year terms, and representatives are elected to two-year terms. Voters in each of Alaska's legislative districts elect one or two legislators, depending on the population in that district. Every ten years, after the federal census is taken, the boundaries of Alaska's legislative districts are redrawn. This assures that the state's legislators are fairly representing the citizens.

Alaska's governor is the state's chief executive. Voters elect the governor and the lieutenant governor to four-year terms. The governor can serve only two terms in a row, but the lieutenant governor can serve any number of terms. The governor administers, or oversees, all the state's executive departments and appoints commissioners to head them. These departments include education, environmental conservation, health and social services, law, military affairs, transportation, and natural resources.

The state's judicial system consists of several levels of courts. The state supreme court is Alaska's highest court. It has the final authority over all lower-court cases that are appealed. The governor appoints the five supreme-court justices, who then select one of their members as chief justice. Alaska's three-member court of appeals hears appeals of criminal cases from the superior court. The superior court tries serious criminal and civil cases, hears domestic-relations cases, and takes appeals from district courts. The district courts preside over minor criminal and civil cases.

In 1956, three years before it became a state, Alaska adopted its present constitution. Every ten years, Alaskans vote on whether to retain or replace their constitution. This body of laws can also be amended, or changed, by a two-thirds vote in both houses of the state legislature. Next, a majority of Alaska's voters must approve an amendment. A state constitutional convention may also propose amendments. In this case, too, both the legislature and the people vote on the change. As of 1989, Alaska's constitution had been amended nineteen times.

## LOCAL GOVERNMENT

Alaska's local government is carried out by its cities and organized boroughs. Like the counties in most other states, Alaska's boroughs operate public schools, plan land use, and collect local taxes. Because of Alaska's sparse population, only about one-fifth of the state's area is covered by organized boroughs. The rest of the state is an unorganized borough governed by the state legislature.

City governments, made up of elected mayors and councils, serve Alaska's urban areas and smaller communities. Home-rule cities can make and revise their own local laws. One Alaskan

The University of Alaska has campuses in Fairbanks (left), Anchorage, and Juneau.

community, Metlakatla, was organized as a city by federal law. Once a Tsimshian Indian reservation, Metlakatla can now provide its residents with city services.

## EDUCATION

Alaskans are among the best-educated people in the country. Eighty-three percent of all adults in Alaska are high-school graduates, compared to the national average of 67 percent. College graduates comprise 21 percent of Alaska's population, while the average nationwide is 16 percent.

State law requires all children in Alaska to attend school from age seven through age fifteen. About 100,000 students are enrolled in Alaska's 480 public schools. Over 40 percent of those students are in the Anchorage school district. Approximately 4,500 students attend private elementary and secondary schools. Until 1985, the United States Bureau of Indian Affairs (BIA) also operated schools in Alaska.

A one-room schoolhouse in Savoonga, on Saint Lawrence Island

Thanks to Molly Hootch, a student from Emmonak, all high-school-age students in Alaska are entitled to attend public schools in their own village. Until 1976, Molly and many other students in small Alaskan communities had to travel to high schools in neighboring villages. In 1976, a lawsuit filed on Molly's behalf led to the so-called Molly Hootch Decree. This act provides for a state-supported secondary school in any community with at least one high-school-age student.

Tiny, one-room schoolhouses are found in many remote Alaskan villages. Since 1939, children in Alaska have been able to study at home and receive their education through state-sponsored correspondence courses. Today, more than 800 students throughout Alaska are enrolled in home-study programs.

The University of Alaska, which first opened in 1922, now enrolls about 30,000 students per year. Its three divisions are in Fairbanks, Anchorage, and Juneau. Community colleges, extension centers, and research facilities are found throughout the state. Alaska's private colleges include Alaska Pacific University, in Anchorage; Sheldon Jackson College, in Sitka; and Alaska Bible College, in Glennallen.

## EMPLOYMENT

Alaska's largest employer is government. In fact, Alaska ranks first among the states in government employment. Over 30 percent of Alaska's workers hold federal, state, or local government jobs, including those on military bases. Government employment is highest in the large cities and in the native villages.

About 20 percent of Alaska's labor force is engaged in service industries such as social and health services, education, hotels, entertainment, and repairs. The wholesale and retail trades employ another 20 percent. Other Alaskans work in the transportation, communication, and utilities industries; manufacturing industries; and the finance, insurance, and real estate industries.

Alaska's unemployment rate is generally slightly higher than the national average. However, much of the unemployment is due to Alaska's seasonal employment patterns. During the summer months, many more workers are hired for fishing, timber harvesting, and construction jobs than in the winter.

## REGIONAL ECONOMIES

With its wide diversity of geographic features, natural resources, and settlement patterns, Alaska has not just one state economy but several.

North and west of the Yukon River, the production of oil and gas and the mining of zinc and gold are the predominant economic activities. In the Yukon and Kuskokwim river valleys, Bristol Bay, Kodiak, the Alaska Peninsula, and the Aleutian and Pribilof islands, fishing is the major commercial activity. Government employment dominates the interior, especially in

**Fishing is one of the major economic activities in the southeast, and agriculture is important in the Matanuska Valley.**

Fairbanks, where 40 percent of the city's workers have government jobs. The principal economic activities in the southeast are logging, pulp production, fishing, mining, and tourism.

Alaska's south-central region has the most balanced economy in the state. With about 60 percent of Alaska's total population, this region includes Anchorage, the Matanuska and Susitna river valleys, the Kenai Peninsula, and Valdez-Cordova. Industries here include oil and natural gas production, fishing and seafood processing, agriculture, government, finance, construction, and tourism.

### MINING AND MINERALS

Mining accounts for about 14 percent of Alaska's gross state product. The gross state product is the total value of all the goods and services produced in the state in a year. Oil and natural gas are the state's most valuable mining products. They bring in more

**Tourists spend about $700 million in Alaska each year. These cruise ship passengers are viewing Misty Fiords.**

than half of Alaska's state government revenues, or income. Over 90 percent of Alaska's oil comes from the North Slope oil field near Prudhoe Bay. Alaska ranks first among the states in oil production.

In the late 1980s, gold surpassed sand and gravel as Alaska's second-most-valuable mining product. The Red Dog zinc deposits in the northern region near Kotzebue are the largest unmined zinc reserves in the world. Planned to go into full production in the early 1990s, the Red Dog Mine is owned by the Northwest Arctic Native Association.

Alaska's only commercial coal mine is the Usibelli Mine, in Healy. Natural gas has increasingly replaced coal as a heating fuel. However, Japan and other Asian nations purchase Alaskan coal to use in their steel mills.

The Greens Creek Mine in the southeast is the nation's largest silver-producing mine. Antimony, mercury, platinum, tin, tungsten, lead, jade, and soapstone are some of Alaska's other minerals.

## FISHERIES

Alaska leads the nation in the value of its seafood catch. The state's annual seafood harvest is worth over $1.8 billion to its fisheries. Prepared and processed, that same seafood sells for about $3 billion in wholesale markets.

Alaska's fisheries are also the state's largest private employers. After the oil industry, the seafood industry provides the greatest revenues to the state's treasury.

Salmon is the most valuable of the state's fish, accounting for about half of the industry's income. Sockeye, chum, pink, coho, and king salmon are the leading species, with Cordova, Bristol Bay, and Cook Inlet as the heaviest salmon-fishing areas.

Next in economic importance are groundfish, or bottom dwellers. Pollock, Pacific cod, sablefish (black cod), rockfish, flatfish, Atka mackerel, and ocean perch are the state's more important groundfish species.

Other important commercial fish are halibut, herring, and smelt. Alaskan shellfish catches include king, tanner (snow), and Dungeness crabs, which are caught in wire-mesh pots.

## FORESTRY AND FURS

The Tongass National Forest in the southeast region provides almost all the state's timber products. Sawmills in Annette and Wrangell cut logs into lumber for export. At pulp mills in Ketchikan and Sitka, wood is chipped, dissolved, and compressed into wood pulp. The pulp is then sold in both United States and foreign markets.

Once Alaska's only commercial industry, the Alaskan fur industry today brings in between $5 million and $10 million a

Alaska leads the nation in the value of its seafood catch, and its forest-products industry has a value of about $350 million per year.

year. Fur seals in the Pribilof Islands provide about 70 percent of Alaska's fur income. Seal hunting is controlled by the federal government, however, to preserve the seal herds.

Alaskan trappers also catch beavers, coyotes, red and Arctic foxes, lynxes, martens, minks, and raccoons for their pelts. Hunting and trapping of all these animals is controlled by state law.

## AGRICULTURE

About 1.4 million acres (566,566 hectares) of Alaskan land— less than one-half of 1 percent of the state's total land area— is classified as farmland. Crops cover about 17,000 acres (6,880 hectares) of the farm acreage, while the rest is either pastureland or unused land.

Crops account for about two-thirds of Alaska's agricultural income, while livestock and poultry products provide the remaining one-third. Milk, however, is the state's most valuable agricultural product. Next in order are hay, potatoes, beef and veal, silage, and reindeer meat and by-products. Other important farm products are vegetables, eggs, barley, pork, and oats.

About 70 percent of Alaska's farm output comes from the fertile Matanuska-Susitna Valley north of Anchorage. Farmers in the valley raise dairy cattle, feed crops, and vegetables.

Over 20 percent of the state's farm products come from the Tanana Valley, near Fairbanks. The state's other farming regions include the Kenai Peninsula, Kodiak and the Aleutian islands, and the southeast.

## MANUFACTURING

Alaska's natural resources provide most of the raw materials for the state's manufacturing industries. Accounting for about 4 percent of the gross state product, Alaska's manufactured goods include food products, especially those made from fish, and wood products. The state's major seafood-processing activity is canning salmon. Plants also smoke, salt, freeze, or package halibut, herring, sablefish, king and Dungeness crab, and other seafood items. Round logs, lumber, wood pulp, and paper products are Alaska's major wood products.

Other goods manufactured in the state are electrical and nonelectrical machinery, construction materials made from sand and gravel, computer equipment, and handcrafted items.

## TRANSPORTATION

Because of Alaska's populated coastal areas and its rugged terrain, the state's major transportation systems are water and air

A seaplane brings in supplies for Huslia in the interior.

routes. Ferries in the Alaska Marine Highway System carry more than 350,000 passengers and 92,000 vehicles a year.

Alaska has been called the "flyingest" state in the Union. There are more people with pilot licenses in Alaska than in any other state. One of every forty-nine Alaskans is licensed to fly. Bush pilots can land their small aircraft in the most rugged, wooded, marshy, and mountainous areas.

Alaska has about 750 airports, heliports, and seaplane landing sites, as well as an international airport in Anchorage. Jets flying the polar route—across the North Pole between Europe, Asia, and North America—often refuel in Anchorage. With the opening of Soviet air space, Anchorage's international air traffic enjoys shorter flight times by following the great circle route from Europe and Asia to Anchorage.

Alaska's first road, running between Valdez and Eagle, dates from the gold-rush days of the late 1800s. It was named the

**Motorists on the Richardson Highway can enjoy this view of the Worthington Glacier at Thompson Pass.**

Richardson Military Trail in 1901. Now extended and paved, the Richardson Highway follows the route of the Alaska Pipeline between Valdez and Fairbanks.

At Delta Junction, the Richardson joins the Alaska Highway, the major land route from Alaska to Canada and the Lower 48. Only 298 miles (480 kilometers) of the Alaska Highway is in Alaska. The rest of its 1,422-mile (2,288-kilometer) length extends through Canada to Dawson Creek, British Columbia.

Another important Alaskan roadway is the Dalton Highway, or North Slope Haul Road, which parallels the pipeline from Fairbanks to Prudhoe Bay. The Glenn, George Parks, Haines, Klondike, Sterling, and Seward highways are some of Alaska's other major land routes. Because of winter weather conditions, much of Alaska's 8,700 miles (14,001 kilometers) of roads are closed from November through March.

About 550 miles (885 kilometers) of rail lines run through Alaska's interior. Passengers can ride the state-owned Alaska Railroad between Anchorage and Fairbanks.

Alaska Railroad lines run between Anchorage and Fairbanks.

## COMMUNICATION

The *Sitka Times*, first published in Sitka in 1868, was Alaska's first newspaper. Today, the state's major daily newspapers are the *Anchorage Daily News*, the *Anchorage Times*, the Fairbanks *Daily News Miner*, the *Ketchikan Daily News*, the *Sitka Daily Sentinel*, and the *Juneau Empire*. Alaskans publish about eighty other newspapers and periodicals.

Radio broadcasts are a vital source of information for people in remote areas of Alaska. Local radio waves convey weather information for fishermen and hunters, as well as emergency communications and personal messages. In all, Alaska has about sixty-two AM and FM radio stations.

Alaska's first television stations, KTVA and KFIA, began broadcasting from Anchorage in 1953. For many years, television was available only in large cities such as Anchorage and Fairbanks. Television finally came to the bush in the late 1970s, with the construction of satellite-transmission receiving stations. Now Alaska has about fourteen public and commercial television stations.

Chapter 8

# RECREATION
# AND CULTURE

# RECREATION AND CULTURE

While ice, snow, and frigid temperatures may discourage recreation in the Lower 48, fun-loving Alaskans enjoy themselves all year round. With their unique climate, terrain, history, and culture, Alaskans have devised some sports of their own, as well as Alaskan versions of traditional entertainments.

## DOG MUSHING

Dog mushing, or sled-dog racing, is Alaska's official state sport. Once a major means of transportation in Alaska, sled-dog teams have been gradually replaced by mechanical snow machines that now haul loads through the snow. Still, hundreds of Alaskans keep sled dogs for working, for racing, or simply for the pleasure of mushing through the snow.

Dog-mushing races in Alaska run the gamut from community club-sponsored events to world championships with prizes as high as $50,000. A championship dog team may consist of as many as sixteen dogs. However, not all these dogs finish the race. Like human runners, racing dogs may suffer from aching muscles or tired feet.

Some of the more important races include the World Championship Sled Dog Races, held every February in Anchorage, and the North American Open Sled Dog Championship, held in Fairbanks every March. Other championship races include the Yukon Quest International Sled Dog Race, the All-Alaska Sweepstakes, and the Alaska State

Championship Race. The most famous dog-mushing event of them all, however, is the Iditarod.

## THE LAST GREAT RACE ON EARTH

Alaska's Iditarod Trail Sled Dog Race, known more simply as the Iditarod, has been called the "Last Great Race on Earth." Stretching from Anchorage to Nome, the Iditarod follows parts of two former dog-team mail routes, one from Seward to Iditarod and the other from Fairbanks to Nome. Part of the latter trail made the headlines in 1925, when Nome was threatened by a diphtheria epidemic. Mushers rushed diphtheria serum from Nenana to Nome, saving the town from disaster.

In honor of Alaska's position as the forty-ninth state, Alaskans often declare the length of the trail to be 1,049 miles (1,688 kilometers). However, its true length is closer to 1,100 miles (1,770 kilometers).

A short version of the Iditarod was organized in 1967, and in 1973 a full-length, Anchorage-to-Nome race was held. The race has continued every year since then. In 1976, the United States Congress declared the Iditarod route a National Historic Trail.

Iditarod mushers start out from downtown Anchorage on the first Saturday of every March. Taking from ten days to three weeks, they cross the Alaska and Kuskokwim mountain ranges, tear through frozen muskeg swamps, and dash across ice on frozen Norton Sound. Cash prizes as high as $50,000 await the first twenty mushers who complete the race.

Susan Butcher won the Iditarod in 1986, 1987, 1988, and 1990. She and musher Rick Swenson are the race's only four-time winners. Joe Redington, who helped organize the 1967 race, continues to compete successfully. Other past champions, each

Musher Susan Butcher won the 1990 Iditarod to
become the second four-time winner of the race.

with a following of fans, include Libby Riddles—the first woman
to win the race (1985)—and two-time winner Dick Mackey.

## WINTER GAMES, SKATING, AND SKIING

Since 1970, athletes from Alaska, northern Alberta, the Yukon
Territory, and the Northwest Territories have come together to
compete in the Arctic Winter Games. The games, held in March of
even-numbered years in either Alaska or Canada, include such
Arctic sports as ice hockey, cross-country (Nordic) skiing, curling,
figure skating, speed skating, a snowshoe/bow-and-arrow
biathlon, and a speed-skating/skiing/snowshoeing triathlon.

The United States Olympic Committee nominated Anchorage as
the site for the 1994 Olympic Winter Games. Although the city
was not chosen, Alaskans are proud of Anchorage's Olympic-class
sports facilities and its natural surroundings. Anchorage's
Sullivan Arena has an Olympic-sized ice arena perfect for speed

skating, figure skating, and ice hockey. Kincaid Park, south of downtown Anchorage, can easily accommodate cross-country skiing/bow-and-arrow biathlon events. In 1983, the park hosted the Cross-Country World Cup competition. Bobsled and luge events are possible at Eagle River, a few miles north of Anchorage.

Many competitive cross-country skiing events are held in Alaska each year. The United States Olympic cross-country ski team practices at Hatcher Pass. The Alaska Nordic Ski Cup Series is held in Anchorage, Fairbanks, Homer, and Salcha. Winners go on to compete in the Arctic Winter Games and the Junior Olympics.

Noncompetitive downhill (Alpine) and cross-country (Nordic) skiers also delight in Alaska's natural ski slopes and powdery trails. The state's largest ski area is Alyeska Resort, southeast of Anchorage on 3,939-foot (1,201-meter) Mount Alyeska. The Eaglecrest Ski Area, on Douglas Island near Juneau, hosts the Rainier Skiing Challenge Cup for downhillers every year.

Good locations for cross-country skiing in Alaska are nearly unlimited, with excellent cross-country trails at the Eaglecrest Ski Area, Chugach State Park, Turnagain Pass, and Chena Hot Springs. Rugged cross-country adventurers enjoy the challenge of Tongass National Forest's wilderness terrain.

## TEAM SPORTS

Basketball is a popular spectator sport in Alaska. At Thanksgiving, some of the finest college basketball teams in the country converge on Anchorage's Sullivan Arena to compete in the Great Alaska Shootout. In February, the University of Alaska-Anchorage hosts the Northern Lights Women's Invitational Basketball Tournament.

Alaskan fans enjoy cheering both college and visiting professional hockey teams that face off in the state's arenas. It's easy for Alaskans to get involved in a hockey game, too. Amateurs manage to get games going on frozen lakes or city rinks.

Alaska does not immediately come to mind when one thinks of baseball. Nevertheless, the national sport is very much alive in the state. Eight Alaskan amateur-league teams make up the Alaska Baseball League. Alaskan teams have won nine National Baseball Congress championships since 1968. Scouts have picked more than 150 Alaskan Leaguers to go on to the major leagues. Baseball stars such as Tom Seaver, Chris Chambliss, and Dave Winfield all played for a brief time in the Alaska League.

## PARKLANDS

Visitors to Alaska's national and state parklands can indulge in hiking, canoeing, fishing, mountain climbing, bird-watching, wildlife watching, and many other outdoor activities.

Massive Mount McKinley towers over Denali National Park and Preserve, the most famous of Alaska's fifteen national parks and preserves. Ambitious mountain climbers can attempt the climb, while wildlife watchers enjoy the park's caribou, Arctic foxes, grizzly bears, Dall sheep, and moose. In Katmai National Park and Preserve, hikers can trek the barren, volcanic landscape of the Valley of the Ten Thousand Smokes. Glacier Bay National Park and Preserve, usually toured by boat, contains some of the world's most stunning glaciers. North of the Arctic Circle, and straddling the Brooks Range, is Gates of the Arctic National Park and Preserve, with forestland, frozen tundra, and the North Slope's "polar desert." The state's two national forests are the Chugach, in the south-central region, and the Tongass, in the southeast.

These Eskimos at Nome are demonstrating a blanket toss.

Alaska's state park system oversees about one hundred parks, recreation areas, historic sites, and state trails. These include Chilkat Bald Eagle Preserve, near Haines; Totem Bight State Historical Park, near Ketchikan; Baranof Castle Hill State Historical Site, in Sitka; and Denali and Chugach state parks.

## FESTIVALS, CELEBRATIONS, AND AMUSEMENTS

Alaskans love to celebrate. Their history, their wilderness terrain, their native cultures, and even their long winter season have become causes for celebration. Unique to Alaska is the "rondy," short for *rendezvous*—an occasion for people to come together and enjoy each other for a while. Several towns have an annual rondy, featuring races, games, sporting events, craft exhibits, and food.

Many Eskimo festivals in Alaska feature blanket tosses as an entertaining spectacle. The blanket toss did not originate as an entertainment, however. Using walrus skins, Eskimos used to toss hunters into the air to spot faraway game. Some were tossed as high as 20 feet (6 meters) into the air.

The Anchorage Fur Rendezvous, or Fur Rondy, called the Mardi Gras of the North, draws crowds from all over the world. Originally organized by fur trappers to break the midwinter boredom, the February event is now one of the biggest winter festivals in the nation. Participants enjoy more than a hundred activities, including car racing, fur auctions, blanket tosses, a costume ball, and the World Championship Sled Dog Races.

Juneau celebrates its gold-mining days every February with the Taku Rondy festival. This boisterous celebration features seafood feasts, dance-hall music, and a ragtime piano-playing contest.

On Alaska Day, in mid-October, Sitka celebrates the day the United States acquired Alaska from Russia. Citizens reenact the 1867 transfer ceremony and dress up in nineteenth-century garb for a costume ball. Adding ethnic color, the New Archangel Dancers perform Russian dances.

Alaska's Russian heritage is perhaps most apparent on Kodiak Island. Every January, the people of Kodiak hold a Russian Orthodox Masquerade Ball and a Russian New Year celebration.

Ice is the basis for an amazing array of events in Alaska. Every spring, contestants converge on Nenana for the Nenana Ice Classic. Whoever guesses the exact time that the ice in the Tanana River breaks up wins a hefty cash prize.

Another ice-related festival is Nome's Bering Sea Ice Classic Golf Tournament. To take part in this lighthearted competition on the frozen Bering Sea, no previous golf experience is required. In February, Valdez welcomes adventurous climbers to its annual International Ice Climbing Festival. At about the same time, Cordova holds an Iceworm Festival as a humorous tribute to these tiny creatures that crawl on glaciers.

The village of Savoonga, on Saint Lawrence Island, holds a Walrus Festival in May. In Barrow, North America's

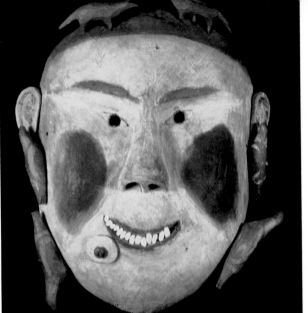

Among the articles produced by Alaska's native artisans are (clockwise from bottom left) Tlingit masks, Athabascan mittens, Inuit masks, and Chilkat blankets.

northernmost community, residents celebrate the end of the year with their Christmas Qitiks (festival). Anyone may participate in the activities, which include a golf tournament, dog races, mukluk (snow-boot) races, Eskimo games, and dancing.

## ARTS AND CRAFTS

Alaska's Indians and Eskimos, relying on centuries-old artistic traditions, produce ceramics, textiles, carvings, prints, and many other handcrafted items. Much of Alaska's nonnative artwork features distinctive native designs, as well.

The Alaska Indian Arts center in Haines is one of the major native arts and crafts centers in the state. Visitors there may observe expert native artisans at work. Eskimos gather in Nome and Kotzebue every summer to market their exquisite ivory carvings, as well as handmade baskets and dolls.

One of the most stunning native art forms in Alaska is the totem pole. Carved from cedar logs, the totems stand up to 80 feet (24 meters) high. Today, skilled craftspeople train with master carvers to produce totem poles just as other artisans did hundreds of years ago.

Several Alaska towns host art shows, and museums throughout the state exhibit both native and nonnative works of art. Fine collections of Alaskan art can be found in the University of Alaska Museum, in Fairbanks; the Alaska State Museum, in Juneau; the Anchorage Museum of History; and in many smaller museums.

## PERFORMING ARTS

Both Western and native music, theater, and dance are represented in Alaska's performing arts. The city of Anchorage boasts a symphony orchestra and the Anchorage Opera. The Fairbanks Concert Association, the University of Alaska-Fairbanks music department, and the Juneau Symphony Orchestra also offer a number of classical performances during their regular seasons.

Juneau's Perseverance Theatre is nationally known for its innovative productions. The Fairbanks Drama Association, the Fairbanks Light Opera Theatre, the University of Alaska-Fairbanks Drama Workshop, and the Anchorage Repertory Theatre present a variety of theater productions each year.

**The internationally known Chilkat Dancers perform at Port Chilkoot, near Haines.**

In the Tlingit village of Saxman, native performers present their customs, history, myths, and songs at the Naa Kahidi Theater. There, the traditions that the Tlingits, Haidas, and Tsimshians once passed from generation to generation have flowered into rich performances reflecting their age-old ways.

Various troupes around the state present colorful native dances. Visitors may be entertained by the internationally known Chilkat Dancers in Haines or the Cape Fox Dancers in Saxman. Eskimos present traditional dances at the Living Museum of the Arctic, in Kotzebue. Fairbanks's annual Festival of Native Arts also features native dancers. Sitka's New Archangel Dancers are known for their lively performances reflecting Alaska's Russian heritage.

Chapter 9
# A TOUR OF
# THE LAST FRONTIER

# A TOUR OF THE LAST FRONTIER

It would take many visits—many years, really—to take in all the wonders that make up Alaska. This tour touches on the highlights of the Last Frontier, from the mild southeast to the frozen Arctic.

## THE SOUTHEAST

"If you don't like the weather," southeasterners like to say, "wait five minutes." With the Coast Mountains on the east and warm Pacific Ocean waters on the west, the climate here changes rapidly. Rain, fog, and chilly breezes come and go, so travelers are advised to dress in layers that they can shed.

Alaska's southeast is a natural wonderland of islands, glaciers, fjords, and forests. No highways connect the Panhandle's cities; instead, people travel along the Alaska Marine Highway, a system of ferries that run up and down along the Panhandle.

Winding through the islands of the Alexander Archipelago up to Skagway is a well-traveled channel called the Inside Passage. One-fourth of all tourists to Alaska are passengers on cruise ships along this breathtaking scenic passage.

On the far south end of the Panhandle is Ketchikan, the first Alaskan stop for travelers along the Inside Passage. Killer whales leaping into the air are a common sight in Ketchikan's waters. Calling itself the Salmon Capital of the World, Ketchikan harbors an array of salmon and halibut fleets. In town, the Tongass Historical Society Museum houses native and pioneer artifacts.

**The Indian tribal house at Totem Bight State Park, in Ketchikan**

By boat or plane out of Ketchikan, one can visit the breathtaking fjords and plentiful wildlife of Misty Fiords National Monument.

In and around Ketchikan is the largest collection of totem poles in the world. Totems in Saxman Indian Village, Totem Bight State Historical Park, and the Totem Heritage Center give a dramatic insight into this centuries-old native art form.

Hyder, north of Ketchikan and sharing the headwaters of the Portland Canal with the Canadian town of Stewart, is called the "friendliest ghost town in Alaska." Remnants of old mines lie along the mountain trails, and Hyder's museum tells heartbreaking tales of early prospectors. At the Glacier Inn, visitors can follow the old miners' tradition of signing a dollar bill and tacking it to the wall. This was to insure against coming back to town broke. Bills from countries all over the world now paper the inn's walls. Helicopter and bus tours out of Hyder reveal more than twenty glaciers, including the glistening, sapphire-blue Bear Glacier.

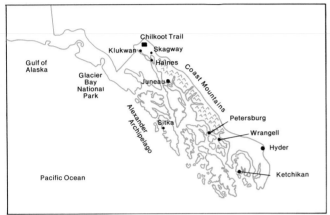

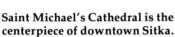

**Saint Michael's Cathedral is the centerpiece of downtown Sitka.**

Up the Panhandle from Ketchikan is Wrangell, the only town in Alaska to have served under the Russian, British, and American flags. Mountains, fjords, and forests surround this island community that hosted prospectors in three gold rushes. Today, visitors to Wrangell marvel at mysterious petroglyphs (ancient rock carvings) visible along its beach at low tide. A collection of Tlingit totem poles surrounds Chief Shakes tribal house on an island in Wrangell's harbor.

Petersburg, on Mitkof Island in the center of the Panhandle, calls itself Little Norway. Rosemaling, a Norwegian flower-painting art, adorns the town's homes and storefronts.

Sitka, the historic Russian-American capital on Baranof Island, is rich in both Russian and Tlingit cultures. Within Sitka National Historical Park is a wildlife sanctuary, a cultural center for Indian

**Alaska's capital city of Juneau has been called the longest city in the world.**

and Russian history and art, and a Tlingit totem park. On Castle Hill, once a Tlingit settlement, the American flag was first raised over Alaska in 1867. Topped by an onion-shaped dome, Saint Michael's Orthodox Cathedral holds a beautiful collection of icons, or religious paintings.

Alaska's capital of Juneau, called the longest city in the world, stretches some 40 miles (64 kilometers) along the shore. At the gateway to Glacier Bay, Juneau nestles between lofty Mount Juneau and Gastineau Channel.

Juneau's downtown landmarks include the Alaska State Capitol, with four pillars of southeastern Alaskan marble. At the head of Seward Street stands a famous totem. Touching the totem, according to local tradition, brings good fortune. Saint Nicholas Russian Orthodox Church, built in 1894, is Alaska's oldest Russian church. Wickersham House, home of Judge James Wickersham, is now a museum filled with fabulous memorabilia he collected on his travels through Alaska. Exhibits in the Alaska State Museum range from stuffed brown bears to modern art.

**Mendenhall Glacier, in Glacier Bay National Park**

By helicopter from Juneau, "flightseers" can soar over magnificent Mendenhall Glacier and even land on it and walk around. From the glacier's brittle surface, visitors can gaze down into its deep crevasses and cracks. They can also drink water from a swift glacier stream—one of the best drinks in the world.

Up the Lynn Canal from Juneau is Haines, founded in 1881 as a Presbyterian mission to the native Tlingit people. On the south side of town is the Fort William Henry Seward Historic District, a 1903 fort with several original buildings still intact. Other attractions are the Chilkat Center for the Arts and Alaska Indian Arts, a center where native artisans carve tribal masks, totem poles, and other exquisite sculptures.

On the north side of Haines is the Sheldon Museum and Cultural Center, with exhibits on pioneer history and Tlingit culture. At the commercial boat harbor, passersby can purchase salmon, halibut, and crab fresh from the boats.

Outside of town, the lush wilderness of the Chilkat River Valley lures rafters, glacier climbers, and hikers. Bird-watchers flock to

**Left: A radio-tagged eagle at the Chilkat Bald Eagle Preserve**
**Right: Gold-rush-era buildings along Skagway's seven-block boardwalk**

the Chilkat Bald Eagle Preserve, home to more than 3,500 bald eagles. Klukwan, alongside the Chilkat River, is an active Tlingit village.

Farther north is Skagway, whose points of interest center around its colorful past. Shops and saloons along Skagway's seven-block boardwalk either date from the gold-rush days or were built in the period's style. The granite Trail of '98 Museum, erected in 1899 as the McCabe College for Women, exhibits gold-rush artifacts and native cultural displays. In the Gold Rush Cemetery are casualties of the town's rougher days. There, for instance, lie notorious citizens Soapy Smith and Frank Reid, who shot each other in a duel in 1898. A twenty-thousand-piece mosaic of driftwood forms the false front of Skagway's Arctic Brotherhood Hall, once a pioneers' meeting hall.

Hardy hikers follow prospectors' footsteps along the 33-mile (53-kilometer) Chilkoot Trail, now part of the Klondike Gold Rush National Historical Park. By air, "flightseers" can survey spectacular Glacier Bay National Park.

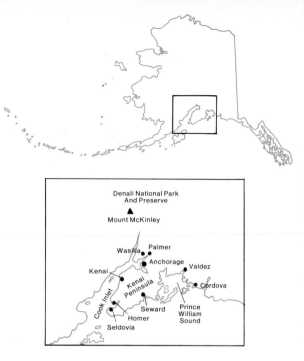

Denali National Park
And Preserve
▲
Mount McKinley

Wasilla  Palmer
Anchorage  Valdez
Kenai
Kenai
Peninsula
Cook Inlet
Cordova
Seward  Prince
Homer  William
Seldovia  Sound

**Downtown Anchorage at twilight**

## SOUTH-CENTRAL ALASKA

Rising in sharp contrast to the surrounding wilderness are the
luxury hotels, restaurants, and shopping districts of Anchorage,
Alaska's largest city. From many of Anchorage's gleaming office
buildings, executives of major oil companies oversee the state's
massive oil-production activities.

It was the state oil revenues that financed Project 80s, the
largest construction program in Anchorage's history. Out of this
project came Anchorage's new Performing Arts Center, George M.
Sullivan Sports Arena, William A. Egan Civic and Convention
Center, and Z. J. Loussac Public Library. The project also
expanded the Anchorage Museum of History and Art, which
houses a magnificent collection of Alaskan art and history
exhibits. Children enjoy the museum's children's section, as well
as the Imaginarium, a hands-on science museum.

On the west side of town is the 1915 Oscar Anderson House, the city's first permanent wood-frame structure. One of the attractions outside the downtown area is Earthquake Park, its shattered landscape a dramatic reminder of the 1964 earthquake. North of the downtown area is Elmendorf Air Force Base.

In south Anchorage, along Cook Inlet's Turnagain Arm, the Seward Highway passes Alyeska Ski Resort. Nearby is the old mining town of Girdwood, which moved 2.1 miles (3.4 kilometers) up the road during the 1964 earthquake! Farther along the Seward Highway, at the head of Turnagain Arm, visitors can learn about the formation of glaciers and the area's natural history at the Begich-Boggs Visitor Center. Portage Glacier is about three miles from the center.

The Seward Highway continues south to the Kenai Peninsula, terminating in Seward, at the head of Resurrection Bay. Tours of the bay highlight the fjords on its west bank. Most of the Kenai Peninsula is national parkland. The Kenai National Wildlife Refuge is known for its vast moose range and its canoe trails. Homer, on Kachemak Bay, is a picturesque art colony. In Seldovia, across the bay from Homer, is a famous onion-domed Russian church. The Russian church in Kenai, an important oil center on Cook Inlet, is one of the finest in the state. Just outside of Kenai is Soldotna, another historic Russian settlement.

Southeast of Anchorage, the Chugach National Forest rims Prince William Sound. Ferries along the sound provide access to the communities of Cordova and Valdez. Cordova lies near the mouth of the Copper River, known for its salmon as well as its migratory birds. Valdez, the southern end of the Trans-Alaska Pipeline, was largely rebuilt after the 1964 earthquake.

East of Anchorage, the Eagle River marks the entrance to Chugach State Park, where moose and bears roam freely. Visitors

**Brightly painted spirit houses mark the graves of this Athabascan burial ground in the Indian village of Eklutna.**

can keep dangerous animals away by making loud noises as they travel the park's trails. Farther north, in the Indian village of Eklutna, is Saint Nicholas Russian Orthodox Church, the oldest building in the Anchorage area. Brightly painted Dena'ina spirit houses stand nearby, marking the graves of an Athabascan burial ground.

Northeast of Anchorage along the Glenn Highway is Palmer, home of the Museum of Alaska Transportation and Industry and the annual Alaska State Fair. A few miles east of Palmer, just south of Glenn Highway, motorists can view the magnificent Matanuska Glacier.

North of Anchorage on the George Parks Highway is Wasilla, headquarters for the annual Iditarod and home of the Mushers Hall of Fame. Farther north, near Willow, is the Independence Gold Mine. Once an active mine, it is now a state park where visitors enjoy horseback riding, picnicking, and hiking. Continuing on to the Talkeetna area, one arrives at Denali State

Mount McKinley, the highest peak in North America, is the crowning point of Denali National Park.

Park, the jumping-off point for many climbing expeditions to Mount McKinley.

Denali National Park and Preserve, northwest of the state park, is one of Alaska's most visited spots. Formerly Mount McKinley National Park, its name was changed in 1980 to Denali, the park's Athabascan name, meaning "the high one." Its summit shrouded in clouds, Mount McKinley, the continent's highest peak, is the crowning point of the park. Visitors to the 6 million-acre (2.4 million-hectare) recreation area can also view grizzly bears, caribou, Dall sheep, foxes, moose, and many other wildlife species. Backpackers, hikers, and campers delight in the park's luxuriously flowered tundra, rushing streams, and forested hills.

## THE SOUTHWEST

Extending southwest toward the Aleutian Islands is the Alaska Peninsula. Here lies the magnificent wilderness of Lake Clark

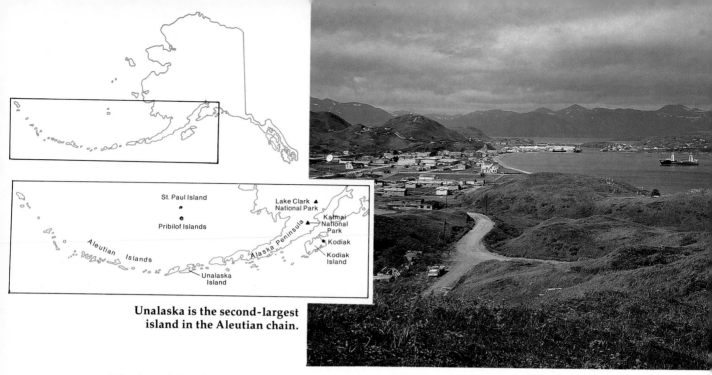

**Unalaska is the second-largest island in the Aleutian chain.**

National Park and Preserve. Farther to the southwest is Katmai National Park and Preserve, a famous habitat for brown bears. Hikers like to trek the park's haunting Valley of the Ten Thousand Smokes.

Kodiak Island, east of the Alaska Peninsula, is the largest of Alaska's thousands of islands. Two-thirds of Kodiak consists of the Kodiak National Wildlife Refuge. About three thousand Kodiak bears, as well as foxes, goats, sea lions, and whales, make their homes here.

Founded in 1792, the town of Kodiak is the state's oldest community. An important commercial fishing center, it is also the sixth-largest city in Alaska. Aleut natives, Russian fur traders, and modern fishermen have all played a part in Kodiak's history. The Baranov Museum, Alaska's oldest structure, contains both Russian and native artifacts. Kodiak's Russian Orthodox Church is another remnant of Russian culture.

On the windswept Aleutian Islands are many fishing ports and wildlife refuges. Unalaska, the second-largest of the chain, can be reached by plane or ferry. The United States Navy maintains a base on Adak Island.

In the Bering Sea north of the Aleutians are the Pribilof Islands. On Saint Paul Island is the largest Aleut community in the world. The Aleuts there depend almost entirely on the island's fur seals for their food and income. The Old Russian Orthodox Church and the old city hall stand as reminders of earlier days. Seal herds and marine birds such as puffins can be seen from cliffs and rookery blinds on the island.

## THE INTERIOR

The frontier spirit is alive in Fairbanks, just as it was in the gold-rush days. Visitors to Fairbanks today can visit a gold camp or take in a spirited saloon show. Passengers on Tanana River steamboats catch a glimpse of the wilderness as the pioneers saw it in the early 1900s. Fairbanks's crisp winter nights are ideal for watching the magnificent northern lights spread across the sky.

Fairbanks offers acres of cross-country ski trails, as well as luge and bobsled runs. Mushing enthusiasts can take sled-dog trips along glistening snow trails outside of town. For the wintertime Ice Festival, ice-carving teams congregate to create fabulous ice sculptures, while mushing fans rally around the North American Open Sled Dog Championship. Fairbanks is also the starting point for the 1,000-mile (1,609-kilometer) Yukon Quest sled-dog race between Fairbanks and Whitehorse in the Yukon Territory.

Every summer, competitors from all over the state participate in Fairbanks's World Eskimo Indian Olympics. Fairbanks's annual Festival of Native Arts celebrates centuries-old native culture.

Eagle, east of Fairbanks on the banks of the Yukon at the Alaska-Canada border, was named for the bald eagles that nested

Fairbanks, which grew up after gold
was discovered there in 1902, is
the trade and transportation center
for Alaska's interior and far north.

on an overlooking bluff. Judge James Wickersham, whose
courthouse is now operated by the Eagle Historical Society, dealt
out justice from his federal bench there. Explorer Roald
Amundsen rushed to Eagle in 1905 to telegraph the news that he
had completed the world's first trip through the Northwest
Passage. Eagle's Roald Amundsen Park commemorates that dog-
mushing expedition.

Prospectors used to bask in the hot springs at Circle, north of
Fairbanks and 50 miles (80 kilometers) below the Arctic Circle.
Before the Dalton Highway to Prudhoe Bay was completed in
1977, Circle was as far north as a highway traveler could go in
Alaska.

Just inside the Arctic Circle, on the northernmost bend of the
Yukon River, lies Fort Yukon. The largest Athabascan village in
the state, Fort Yukon was also the first town in the territory to be
settled by English-speaking people. Fort Yukon's trading posts still
deal in furs and other items.

Athabascan women can be seen around town tanning hides, making moccasins, and fashioning beadwork. In the rustic Episcopal church, Athabascan beadwork adorns the altar cloths, and the hymn books are printed in the Athabascan language.

## THE FAR WEST

On the southern coast of the Seward Peninsula is Nome. About 60 percent of its residents are Eskimos. Great herds of walrus migrate off Nome's shores, and gifted native artists there carve beautiful sculptures from walrus-tusk ivory.

There are two different stories explaining how Nome got its name. According to one, a British ship's officer in the 1850s noticed that a certain spot on a map of Alaska's coast had no name. He wrote "name" next to the spot, and when the map was copied, it was incorrectly transcribed as "Nome." The other story holds that "Nome" comes from the Eskimo phrase *kn-no-me*, meaning "I don't know." This was the Eskimos' reply, so the story goes, when asked the name of that place.

Gold seekers still head for Nome, though not in such numbers as they once did. Nome's beachfront is one of the few areas in Alaska where people can pan for gold without a permit. Nome is also famous as the endpoint for the Iditarod Trail Sled Dog Race. Every March, planeloads of newspeople and other spectators pour into town as Nome celebrates the race with its month-long Iditarod Daze festival.

Kotzebue, discovered by Otto von Kotzebue in 1816, lies north of the Seward Peninsula 30 miles (48 kilometers) within the Arctic Circle. With Inupiat Eskimos making up more than 80 percent of its population, Kotzebue is one of the state's largest and oldest Eskimo communities. Fish-drying racks and handmade fishing boats along the unpaved streets show that many residents still practice traditional subsistence lifestyles. East of Kotzebue is Kobuk Valley National Park. This archaeological site includes two deserts, Great Kobuk Sand Dunes and Little Kobuk Sand Dunes.

At the Living Museum of the Arctic, visitors can hear the famous Kotzebue Eskimo singers and take part in a blanket toss. Visitors can also purchase native craftworks such as soapstone carvings, skin paintings, and masks. At the Jade Mountain Products plant, native artisans fashion jewelry and other items from Alaskan jade.

In early June, when the winter's offshore ice breaks up, beluga (white) whales begin their migration. Eskimos in umiaks and kayaks then take to the sea for their spring whale hunt. Later they drape the whale meat on racks along the streets to dry.

## THE ARCTIC REGION

Alaska's Arctic region is the sparsely populated upper one-fourth of the state. Though the climate is frigid, the tundra supports brilliant Arctic wildflowers and abundant wildlife. This is one of the best regions in the state for viewing the spectacular aurora borealis, or northern lights.

Wilderness parklands in the Brooks Range include Gates of the Arctic National Park and Preserve and Noatak National Preserve. Gates of the Arctic National Park and Preserve covers four times the area of Yellowstone National Park. Within the park's taiga forestland live Athabascan Indians. High in its valleys, Eskimos hunt the native caribou herds.

At the far northern tip of Alaska, Barrow — barren, stark, and desolate — seems to have been strewn on the beach along the Arctic Ocean. This Inupiat Eskimo community, 330 miles (531

Gates of the Arctic National Park covers four times the area of Yellowstone National Park.

kilometers) above the Arctic Circle, is the northernmost settlement in the United States. Although there are no sidewalks, Barrow can be toured on foot or by bus.

Fishing boats and drying racks along the coast are reminders of the local Eskimos' whaling activities. Successful whale hunts in early summer call for whale feasts. Eskimo dances, blanket tosses, and craft markets are part of Barrow's colorful native culture.

Thus ends our tour of the Last Frontier. It has taken us through forests, past volcanoes and glaciers, and across the Arctic plain. Above the horizon we have seen high-rise buildings and one-room native dwellings, towering oil rigs and majestic totem poles. The northern lights have danced across the skies by night, and the midnight sun has shone for months-long days. For the adventurous and the nature lover alike, the splendors of the Great Land still beckon as in ages past.

# FACTS AT A GLANCE

## GENERAL INFORMATION

**Statehood:** January 3, 1959, forty-ninth state

**Origin of Name:** Aleut word *al-ay-es-ka*, meaning "great land" or "mainland"

**State Capital:** Juneau, founded 1880; state capital since 1900

**State Nickname:** Alaska has several unofficial nicknames. They include Last Frontier, Land of the Midnight Sun, and Great Land.

**State Flag:** Alaska's state flag was adopted in 1927, when Alaska was still a territory. The background field of deep blue represents Alaska's sky and the forget-me-not, Alaska's state flower. Seven gold stars in the lower left sector outline the Big Dipper constellation, also known as the Great Bear, a symbol of strength. In the upper right-hand corner is a single gold star, the North Star, representing Alaska's northerly location. The stars' gold color stands for Alaska's gold resources. Benny Benson, a thirteen-year-old schoolboy, designed the flag in 1926 in a competition open to all Alaska schoolchildren.

**State Motto:** North to the Future

**State Bird:** Willow ptarmigan

**State Flower:** Forget-me-not

**State Tree:** Sitka spruce

**State Mineral:** Gold

**State Gem:** Jade

**State Fish:** King salmon

**State Sport:** Dog mushing

**State Fossil:** Mastodon

**State Song:** "Alaska's Flag," words by Marie Drake and music by Elinor Dusenbury, adopted as Alaska's official song in 1955:

Eight stars of gold on a field of blue—Alaska's flag.
May it mean to you the blue of the sea, the evening sky,
The mountain lakes, and the flow'rs nearby;
The gold of the early sourdough's dreams,
The precious gold of the hills and streams;
The brilliant stars in the northern sky,
The "Bear"—the "Dipper"—and, shining high,
The great North Star with its steady light,
Over land and sea a beacon bright.
Alaska's flag—to Alaskans dear,
The simple flag of a last frontier.

# POPULATION

**Population:** 401,851, forty-ninth among the states (1980 census)

**Population Density:** 68 persons per 100 sq. mi. (26 persons per 100 km²)

**Population Distribution:** About 64 percent of Alaskans live in cities or towns, and 36 percent live in rural areas. Forty-three percent of Alaska's people live in Anchorage, the state's largest city.

| | |
|---|---|
| Anchorage | 174,431 |
| Fairbanks | 22,645 |
| Juneau | 19,528 |
| Sitka | 7,803 |
| Ketchikan | 7,198 |
| Kodiak | 4,756 |

(Population figures according to 1980 census)

**Population Growth:** Even though Alaska has the nation's second-smallest state population, its growth rate has been among the highest. The gold rushes of the late 1800s caused the population to nearly double between 1890 and 1900. When the Great Depression struck in the 1930s, many people from the Lower 48 came to Alaska seeking better farming and living conditions. World War II (1939-45) brought an influx of military personnel and civilian workers into the state. With the construction of the Trans-Alaska Pipeline and the start-up of oil production, Alaska's population grew 33 percent during the 1970s. It was projected to increase by at least another 30 percent in the 1980s.

| Year | Population |
|---|---|
| 1880 | 33,426 |
| 1900 | 63,592 |
| 1920 | 55,036 |

| 1940 | 72,524 |
| 1950 | 128,643 |
| 1960 | 226,167 |
| 1970 | 302,583 |
| 1980 | 401,851 |

**Native Peoples:** Alaska's native peoples make up about 16 percent of the state's population. About one-half of these natives are Eskimos and about one-third are Indians; Aleuts make up the smallest group. Alaska's Indians include Athabascan, Tlingit, Haida, and Tsimshian peoples.


# GEOGRAPHY

**Borders:** Alaska is bordered on the east by Canada's provinces of British Columbia and the Yukon Territory. To the north is the Arctic Ocean. The Bering Sea washes Alaska's western shore, and on the south is the North Pacific Ocean and the Gulf of Alaska.

**Highest Point:** Mount McKinley, 20,320 ft. (6,194 m)

**Lowest Point:** Sea level

**Greatest Distances:** North to south—1,350 mi. (2,173 km)
East to west—2,350 mi. (3,782 km)

**Area:** 591,004 sq. mi. (1,530,700 km²)

**Rank in Area Among the States:** First

**Rivers:** More than 3,000 rivers flow through Alaska. The state's longest river is the Yukon, part of which runs through Canada. With a total length of 1,979 mi. (3,185 km), the Yukon is North America's fourth-longest river. The Yukon enters Alaska from Canada's Yukon Territory, flows northwesterly to Fort Yukon, and takes a southwesterly course across the state to its mouth at Norton Sound. Along with its tributaries, the Yukon forms the major drainage system of Alaska's interior. The Koyukuk, the Tanana, and the Porcupine are important tributaries of the Yukon. Alaska's second-longest river is the Kuskokwim, flowing southwesterly from its source in the Alaska Range to Kuskokwim Bay on the Bering Sea. Important rivers in the south are the Susitna, which rises in the Alaska Range, and the Matanuska, which rises in the Chugach Mountains. Both empty into Cook Inlet. The Copper River flows from the Wrangell Mountains to its mouth on the Gulf of Alaska. The major river in the Arctic region is the Colville River, which empties into the Arctic Ocean. Other important rivers in the state include the Innoko, Noatak, Kobuk, Chilkat, Kvichak, Naknek, Nushagak, and Stikine rivers and Birch Creek.

**The Salmon River near Hyder**

**Lakes:** There are more than 3 million lakes in Alaska. Of those, 94 measure larger than 10 sq. mi. (26 km²). Alaska's largest lake is Iliamna Lake, covering about 1,000 sq. mi. (2,590 km²). Other important lakes in the state, in descending order of size, are Becharof, Teshekpuk, Naknek, Tustumena, Clark, Dall, Upper Ugashik, Lower Ugashik, and Kukaklek lakes. Alaska's greatest concentration of lakes occurs in the delta regions of the Yukon and Kuskokwim rivers and the Arctic Slope south of Barrow.

**Topography:** Alaska's major physical regions are the Pacific Mountain System, the Central Plateau, the Rocky Mountain System, and the Arctic Coastal Plain.

The Pacific Mountain System is a continuation of mountain ranges that extend along the Pacific Coast from Alaska to southern California. This arc-shaped chain of peaks covers Alaska's south and southeast region and extends through the Aleutian Islands. Volcanoes, glaciers, and some of the continent's highest peaks, as well as forests and rich farmlands, mark this region. There are two separate groups of mountains in Alaska's Pacific Mountain System. The group nearest the coast is made up of the Saint Elias, Chugach, Wrangell, and Kenai mountains. The other group, arching farther into the mainland, includes the Coast Mountains, the Alaska Range, and the Aleutian Range. North America's highest mountain, Mount McKinley, is the crowning point of the Alaska Range. Mount Saint Elias is the state's second-highest mountain. Fourteen of Alaska's mountains are higher than any other peaks in the United States.

Alaska's Central Plateau, also called the Central Uplands and Lowlands, covers the state's vast interior. This region, lying between the Brooks Range to the north and the Alaska Range to the south, is drained by the Yukon and Kuskokwim river systems. The Kuskokwim Mountains and other low, rolling mountain ranges rise on the Central Plateau, while muskeg swamp covers much of the region's lowlands.

The Rocky Mountain System, or Arctic Mountain System, is made up of the Brooks Range and its foothills. This region is the most northerly extension of North America's Rocky Mountains. Within this system are the Baird, De Long, Davidson, Schwatka, Smith, Romanzof, and Endicott mountains. Peaks in the eastern part of the Brooks Range are generally higher than those in the west.

The Arctic Coastal Plain, or Arctic Slope, is a low plain that slopes down from the Brooks Range northward to the Arctic Ocean. No trees are able to grow here, and the permanently frozen subsoil is known as permafrost. In some areas, a slight thawing of the ground surface permits the growth of wildflowers, mosses, and short grasses. These areas are called tundra.

**Climate:** Alaska's diversity of geographical features results in a variety of climates throughout the state. Southern and southeastern Alaska have milder temperatures than the interior because of warm winds blowing eastward from the Japan Current of the North Pacific Ocean. The average January temperature on the southern coast is about 28° F. (-2° C), and the average in July is about 55° F. (13° C). Although the Aleutian Islands also enjoy mild temperatures, they are plagued by fog, rain, and occasional fierce windstorms called williwaws.

The interior of the state experiences colder winters and warmer summers, with the January average dropping to -9° F. (-23° C) and the July average rising to about 59° F. (15° C). Alaska's record high and low temperatures occurred in the interior. On June 27, 1915, Fort Yukon registered 100° F. (38° C), the state's highest recorded temperature. The lowest temperature ever recorded in Alaska was -80° F. (-62° C), at Prospect Creek on January 23, 1971.

The Arctic region is generally colder than the interior. From the Arctic Coast down to the Seward Peninsula, the seas are frozen for eight to ten months of the year. Nevertheless, the ocean waters warm the air, preventing the extreme temperatures sometimes experienced in the interior. Arctic Alaska averages -11° F. (-24° C) in January and 47° F. (8° C) in July.

Precipitation, or moisture such as rain and snow, also varies greatly throughout the state. Rainfall is heaviest in the southeast, where some spots receive an average of more than 200 in. (508 cm) of rain a year. At Port Walter, on Baranof Island, the average annual precipitation is 221 in. (561 cm) — the highest ever recorded in the continental United States. Barrow, in the far north, receives less than 5 in. (13 cm) of precipitation a year. Alaska's interior averages about 13 in. (33 cm) of precipitation every year. While the southeast receives light snowfalls, the southern coast may receive from 26 in. (66 cm) to 290 in. (737 cm) of snow a year.

# NATURE

**Trees:** Birches, Sitka spruces, white spruces, black spruces, western hemlocks, mountain hemlocks, red cedars, Alaska yellow cedars, lodgepole pines, aspens, cottonwoods, tamaracks, willows

**Polar bears, walruses, and Steller's sea lions are animals native to Alaska.**

**Wild Plants:** Mosses, lichens, ferns, sedges, horsetail, mountain laurels, Arctic daisies, buttercups, bluebells, asters, cinquefoils, fireweeds, forget-me-nots, larkspurs, cowslips, violets, wild hyacinths, wood nymphs, firewood, lupine, shooting stars, anemones, irises, skunk cabbage, bog laurels, labrador tea, cranberries, crowberries, blueberries, raspberries, red currants

**Animals:** Brown bears, Kodiak (Alaskan brown) bears, grizzly bears, black bears, polar bears, wolves, coyotes, red foxes, Arctic foxes, lynxes, moose, caribous, blacktail deer, Dall sheep, mountain goats, elk, musk-oxen, bisons, wolverines, martens, minks, beavers, land otters, sea otters, weasels, muskrats, hares, rabbits, walruses, hair seals, fur seals, Steller's sea lions, bowhead whales, sperm whales, killer whales, beluga whales, porpoises, crabs, shrimp, prawns, clams, scallops

**Birds:** Ducks, geese, swans, cranes, loons, grebes, shearwaters, petrels, albatrosses, jaegers, terns, gulls, murres, murrelets, auklets, guillemots, puffins, plovers, curlews, sandpipers, snipes, grouse, ptarmigans, bald eagles, golden eagles, ravens, magpies, crows, jays, snow buntings, grosbeaks, waxwings, juncos, chickadees

**Fish:** Salmon, cod, herring, halibut, sablefish, rockfish, flatfish, Atka mackerel, ocean perch, flounder, sole, pollock

# GOVERNMENT

Alaska's state government, like the federal government in Washington, D.C., is divided into three branches: legislative, executive, and judicial. The legislature makes the state's laws. It is composed of two houses, a senate and a house of representatives. The twenty state senators are elected from fourteen senate districts to serve four-year terms, and the forty representatives are chosen from twenty-seven election districts for two-year terms.

The governor, as head of the executive branch, enforces the state's laws. The governor and lieutenant governor are elected to four-year terms. An elected governor may not hold more than two consecutive terms in office, but the lieutenant governor may serve for any number of terms. The governor also administers and appoints the heads of important executive departments. These include the departments of administration, commerce and economic development, education, environmental conservation, health and social services, law, military affairs, and transportation.

Alaska's supreme court is the state's highest court. Its five justices select one among them to serve a three-year term as chief justice. The state's second-highest courts are the courts of appeals, with three justices, and the superior court, with twenty-nine justices. Judges for all three courts are appointed by the governor after being nominated by a judicial council. After three years in office, they must be approved by the voters. District courts handle minor criminal and civil matters, as well as municipal cases.

**Number of Counties:** Alaska has no county government. There are thirteen boroughs, whose functions are similar to those of counties in other states.

**U.S. Representatives:** 1

**Electoral Votes:** 3

**Voting Qualifications:** Eighteen years of age, one year state residency, and thirty days residency in the election district

# EDUCATION

Alaska state law requires that all children between the ages of seven and sixteen attend school. About 100,000 students are enrolled in the state's public school system, which operates about 480 elementary and secondary schools. In addition, Alaskan students in kindergarten through twelfth grade have the option of receiving their education through the state's Centralized Correspondence Study Program.

Alaska's first college-level institution was a Russian theological school, opened in Sitka in 1841. In 1915, the United States Congress reserved land in the Tanana Valley for an agricultural and mining college. Finally opened in 1922, the college became the University of Alaska (Fairbanks) in 1935.

Today more than 30,000 students a year enroll in Alaska's public university system. The University of Alaska is now divided into three universities, each with several community campuses. The University of Alaska-Anchorage, the largest division, houses the Alaska Center for International Business and the Institute for Social and Economic Research. At the University of Alaska-Fairbanks are the Alaska Native Language Center, the Geophysical Institute, and other research facilities. Based in Juneau, the University of Alaska-Southeast includes campuses in Sitka and Ketchikan.

Three private institutions are also available to Alaska's college students. They are Alaska Pacific University, in Anchorage; Sheldon Jackson College, in Sitka; and Alaska Bible College, in Glennallen.

## ECONOMY AND INDUSTRY

### Principal Products:

*Agriculture:* Milk, eggs, beef cattle, chickens, hogs, sheep, lambs, reindeer, greenhouse and nursery products, barley, hay, oats, potatoes, cranberries, blueberries, strawberries

*Manufacturing:* Fish and other seafood products, petroleum and coal products, wood products, printed materials, fabricated metal products, construction materials, nonelectrical machinery, clothing, craftwork

*Natural Resources:* Oil, natural gas, forest products, fur pelts, gold, iron ore, tin, barite, copper, mercury, platinum, antimony, nickel, silver, tungsten, uranium, gemstones, lead, molybdenum, zinc, sand, gravel, stone

*Fishing:* Salmon, halibut, sea herring, rockfish, sablefish, smelt, crabs, shrimp, scallops

**Business and Trade:** Federal, state, and local governments are Alaska's largest employers. About 23 percent of the state's gross state product consists of government functions and activities. These include the management of national and state parklands and the staffing of native community organizations.

The mining industry, especially the mining of oil and natural gas, is Alaska's most important production industry. Alaska produces more petroleum than any other state. The state's petroleum revenues provide well over half of Alaska's state government income. The mining of oil, gas, and minerals such as zinc and gold accounts for about 14 percent of Alaska's gross state product. When world oil prices dropped in 1985, the state's petroleum industry suffered a decline, but by the late 1980s the industry was recovering well.

Wholesale and retail trade contribute 13 percent to the gross state product, and social and community services produce another 13 percent. Transportation, communication, and utilities provide 12 percent. Construction, which has fluctuated along with the oil industry, accounts for about 11 percent of the gross state product.

Finance, insurance, real estate, manufacturing, fishing, and agriculture bring in the remaining 14 percent of the gross state product. Although fisheries represent less than 1 percent of Alaska's gross product, they provide the second-greatest revenues to the state's treasury, after the petroleum industry.

In the late 1980s, 72 percent of Alaska's exports—over one billion dollars' worth of goods—went to Japan. Ten percent was exported to Korea, and 5 percent went to China. Fish accounted for 37 percent of Alaska's exports; timber and timber products, 17 percent; and natural gas, 9 percent. Canada supplied 65 percent of Alaska's imported goods, 13 percent came from Japan, and 5.5 percent came from France.

**Communication:** Alaska's major daily newspapers are the *Anchorage Daily News*, the *Anchorage Times*, the Fairbanks *Daily News Miner*, the *Ketchikan Daily News*, the *Sitka Daily Sentinel*, and the *Juneau Empire*. The *Sitka Times*, first published in 1868, was Alaska's first newspaper. Alaskans now publish about eighty other newspapers and periodicals.

Alaska's first radio station, KFQD, began broadcasting from Anchorage in 1924. Today the state has about sixty-two AM and FM radio stations. Some of these are clear-channel stations, having international communications status. Because they bring vital weather information to fishermen and hunters in remote regions, these stations are protected from interference by other stations.

The state's oldest television stations, KTVA and KFIA, began broadcasting from Anchorage in 1953. Only Alaska's large cities had television service until the late 1970s, when satellite-transmission receiving stations brought television reception to the bush. There are now about fourteen public and commercial television stations in Alaska.

**Transportation:** Bush planes, seaplanes, and helicopters provide much of Alaska's interior transportation. The state has about 750 airports, heliports, and seaplane landing sites. Anchorage's international airport is a major refueling point for aircraft flying the polar route between Asia, Europe, and North America. Fairbanks, Juneau, Ketchikan, Kodiak, Sitka, Wrangell, Petersburg, and Nome also have modern airports.

Many of Alaska's coastal towns are most conveniently reached by water. The state's ferry routes cover 1,435 mi. (2,309 km). Ferries in the Alaska Marine Highway System transport more than 350,000 passengers and 92,000 vehicles along the southeast and south-central coasts every year. About 25 percent of Alaska's tourist visitors are passengers of cruise ships along the southeast's Inside Passage.

There are about 8,700 mi. (14,001 km) of roadways in Alaska, of which about 5,742 mi. (9,241 km) are paved. Many of Alaska's roads are closed during the winter because of snow and ice. Most of the state's major highways, however, are open all year. The Richardson Highway, opened to vehicle traffic in 1923, was Alaska's first paved highway. Originally called the Richardson Military Trail, the route began in 1901 as a miners' trail between Valdez and Eagle. It now parallels the Alaska Pipeline between Valdez and Fairbanks. The Dalton Highway follows the pipeline from Fairbanks north to Prudhoe Bay. The Alaska Highway, the major road link from Alaska to Canada and the Lower 48, extends from Dawson Creek, British Columbia, to Fairbanks. Alaska's other major highways include the Denali, Edgerton, George Parks, Glenn, Seward, and Sterling highways.

There are about 550 mi. (885 km) of rail lines in Alaska. The Alaska Railroad, opened in 1923, provides passenger and freight service between Anchorage and Fairbanks. It also offers freight service and limited passenger service as far south as Seward and Whittier. Originally owned by the federal government, the railroad was purchased by the state of Alaska in 1985. The White Pass and Yukon Railroad ran between Whitehorse, in the Yukon Territory, and Skagway from 1900 to 1982. In May 1988, it reopened for excursions only.

## SOCIAL AND CULTURAL LIFE

**Museums:** Alaska's history and culture are richly represented in its many museums and cultural centers. One of the state's major museums is the Alaska State Museum in Juneau, featuring exhibits on natural history, native Alaskan artifacts, mining history, and modern Alaskan art. Visitors here can marvel at stuffed brown bears, a walrus-hide umiak (Eskimo whaling boat), a reconstructed interior of a Tlingit tribal house, and many other displays.

A towering grizzly bear looms over the entrance of the University of Alaska Museum in Fairbanks. This history and natural-science museum is divided into five sections, each highlighting an area in Alaska: the southeast, the interior, the Aleutians, the southwest, and the Arctic. One attraction is Blue Babe, a 38,000-year-old steppe bison that gold miners found mummified in permafrost. The museum also features Native Alaskan works of art, as well as many history and wildlife exhibits.

The Anchorage Museum of History and Art includes both historic and contemporary Alaskan art, Alaskan history displays, and a special children's section.

Sitka's octagonal Sheldon Jackson Museum contains items collected by Dr. Jackson as he pursued his missionary work in remote regions of Alaska. Among the museum's Indian, Eskimo, and Aleut treasures are carved masks, kayaks, dogsleds, Chilkat blankets, and Chief Katlean's helmet from the Tlingits' 1804 battle with the Russians.

The Tongass Historical Museum in Ketchikan displays Indian artifacts and ceremonial objects, as well as mining and fishing items from Alaska's pioneer days. A major totem center, Ketchikan is also home to the Totem Heritage Center, which features authentic ancient totem carvings.

In Kotzebue, Alaska's second-largest Eskimo community, is the Living Museum of the Arctic, one of the state's major museums. The story of the Eskimos' culture and history is told through dioramas and a slide presentation, live dance performances, and an outdoor blanket toss.

The Baranov Museum, in Erskine House on Kodiak Island, was once Alexander Baranov's sea-otter pelt warehouse. Now a museum dedicated to Alaska's Russian days, it displays such articles as Russian samovars and Russian Easter eggs. The Sheldon Museum and Cultural Center, in Haines, contains fascinating Indian and Russian artifacts, as well as memorabilia from gold-rush days.

Among the attractions in Skagway's Trail of '98 Museum are legal documents, saloon artifacts, and gold scales. The Wrangell City Museum features fragments of early totems, petroglyphs, a bootlegger's still, and other historical artifacts. The Iditarod Museum in Wasilla exhibits dogsleds and mushers' gear and shows video

The Alaska State Museum, in Juneau (left), features exhibits on natural history, Alaskan history, mining, and contemporary art. The Totem Heritage Center, in Ketchikan, houses authentic ancient totem carvings (above).

clips from past races. The Museum of Alaska Transportation and Industry, in Palmer, exhibits historic Alaskan transportation equipment, including early aircraft, antique cars, and a sheepherder's wagon. The life and culture of the people of the Yukon Flats are the subject of the Dinjii Zhuu Enjit Museum in Fort Yukon.

Many historic Alaskan homes have been made into museums. The Russian Bishop's House in Sitka, now restored, was built for Bishop Veniaminov in 1842. It is one of the few Russian log buildings still standing in Alaska. Juneau's Wickersham House, built in 1899, was the home of Alaskan judge and congressional delegate James Wickersham. On display there are his forty-seven diaries, Chickering grand piano, and native art pieces. The Oscar Anderson House was Anchorage's first permanent frame house. Butcher Oscar Anderson, who served Anchorage's tent city at the time, built it in 1915.

Other interesting Alaskan museums include the Pratt Museum, in Homer; the Valdez Heritage Center Museum, in Valdez; the Corrington Museum of Alaskan History, in Skagway; the Resurrection Bay Historical Society Museum, in Seward; the Bristol Bay Historical Museum, in Naknek; the Juneau Mining Museum, in Juneau; the Anaktuvuk Pass Museum, in Anaktuvuk Pass; and the Matanuska Valley Museum, in Palmer.

**Libraries:** About ninety public libraries serve Alaska's citizens. In the Alaska State Historical Library in Juneau are many books and documents relating to Alaska's history. The University of Alaska-Fairbanks holds the Rasmuson Library, and the University of Alaska-Anchorage also contains an excellent library. Other libraries in the state include the Z. J. Loussac Library and the Alaska Resources Library, in Anchorage; the Alaska State Archives, in Juneau; and the Jessie Wakefield Memorial Library in Port Lions.

**Performing Arts:** Alaska's performing arts encompass both Western and native music, theater, and dance. Juneau, Anchorage, and Fairbanks support city symphony orchestras. The Anchorage Opera, Fairbanks Concert Association, and University of Alaska-Fairbanks music department also perform classical fare during their regular seasons.

Juneau's Perseverance Theatre is known nationwide for its innovative productions. Other drama groups in the state include the Anchorage Repertory Theatre, the Fairbanks Drama Association, the Fairbanks Light Opera Theatre, and the University of Alaska-Fairbanks Drama Workshop. In the Tlingit village of Saxman, native performers of the Naa Kahidi Theater dramatically present the history, myth, and song of the Tlingit, Haida, and Tsimshian Indians.

Native dances are a major attraction of the Festival of Native Arts, in Fairbanks. Eskimos present traditional dances at the Living Museum of the Arctic, in Kotzebue. The native Cape Fox Dancers perform in Saxman, and the famous Chilkat Dancers entertain visitors in Haines. Sitka's New Archangel Dancers perform colorful Russian dances.

**Sports and Recreation:** The Alaska Baseball League includes eight Alaskan amateur-league teams. Since 1968, Alaskan teams have won nine National Baseball Congress championships.

Alaska has a number of college and amateur basketball and hockey teams. Every February, the University of Alaska-Anchorage hosts the Northern Lights Women's Invitational Basketball Tournament. During Thanksgiving weekend, college basketball teams from all over the country compete in the Great Alaska Shootout at Anchorage's Sullivan Arena.

Downhill (Alpine) and cross-country (Nordic) skiing are popular sports in Alaska. The state hosts several cross-country races, most notably the Alaska Nordic Ski Cup Series.

Dog mushing, or sled-dog racing, is one of Alaska's most unusual sports. Many Alaskans enjoy dog mushing as recreation, while others are serious racers. The most famous dog-mushing race is the Anchorage-to-Nome Iditarod Trail Sled Dog Race, held every March. Other championship races include the World Championship Sled Dog Races, in Anchorage; the North American Open Sled Dog Championship, in Fairbanks; the Yukon Quest International Sled Dog Race, between Fairbanks and Whitehorse; the All-Alaska Sweepstakes, between Nome and Candle; and the Alaska State Championship Race, between Kenai and Soldotna.

Snow machining is another unusual but popular sport in Alaska. Snow machines are indispensable working vehicles for hauling loads through the snow. However, when not on duty, they double as recreational vehicles. Many state parks and recreation areas have snow-machining trails, and snow-machine races are a popular spectator sport.

Alaska's residents and visitors alike enjoy hiking, canoeing, fishing, mountain climbing, bird-watching, and wildlife watching in the many national and state parks. The National Park Service administers fifteen national parklands in Alaska. These include Denali National Park and Preserve (site of Mount McKinley), Bering Land Bridge National Preserve, Glacier Bay National Park and Preserve, Katmai National Park and Preserve, Klondike Gold Rush National Historical Park, and Sitka National Historical Park. The United States Forest Service oversees the

Tongass and Chugach national forests, within which are many recreation areas.

Alaska's state parks are divided into seven park-management districts, which oversee about one hundred areas of different kinds. The state park system includes fifty-six recreation sites, eleven recreation areas, four historic parks, three historic sites, three state trails, five state parks, and one state preserve. State-owned but nonstate-managed areas include Chilkoot Trail, in Skagway; Totem Square, in Sitka; and Valdez Glacier Wayside, in Valdez.

### Historic Sites and Landmarks:

*Baranof Castle Hill State Historical Site*, in Sitka, is the location of the 1867 transfer ceremony during which Alaska passed from Russian to American rule.

*Fort Abercrombie State Historic Park*, near Kodiak, overlooking the Gulf of Alaska, was a heavily manned United States Army post after the Japanese attack on Pearl Harbor during World War II.

*Iditarod National Historic Trail*, between Seward and Nome, was for centuries a major network of trails for both natives and settlers; a segment of the trail is now used for the annual Iditarod Trail Sled Dog Race.

*Independence Mine State Historic Park*, near Palmer, features mine shafts and frame buildings of the high-yielding Independence gold mines, first staked in 1907.

*Klondike Gold Rush National Historical Park*, in the Skagway area and extending into Canada and Washington State, preserves historic buildings from the days of the Klondike gold rush.

*Old Sitka State Historic Site*, near Sitka, established by Aleksandr Baranov in 1799, is the site of the first Russian settlement in southeastern Alaska.

*Rika's Landing State Historic Site*, near Delta Junction, is the site of Rika's Roadhouse, a major shelter for travelers along the gold-rush trail from Valdez to Eagle.

*Sitka National Historical Park*, in Sitka, is the site of the Tlingits' last battle of resistance against the Russian colonizers in 1804.

*Totem Bight State Historical Park*, north of Ketchikan, contains a stunning array of nineteenth-century Tlingit and Haida totem poles.

**Tidewater Glacier, in Glacier Bay National Park**

**Other Interesting Places to Visit:**

*Barrow,* an Inupiat Eskimo community on the Arctic Ocean, is North America's northernmost settlement and a prime location for viewing the midnight sun, which in Barrow does not set for eighty-four days during the summer.

*Chilkat Bald Eagle Preserve,* near Haines, is the meeting place for an estimated 3,500 bald eagles.

*Denali National Park and Preserve,* between Anchorage and Fairbanks, surrounds massive Mount McKinley, North America's highest peak.

*Glacier Bay National Park and Preserve,* near Juneau, features sixteen spectacular glaciers that flow from surrounding mountains.

*Katmai National Park and Preserve,* on the Alaska Peninsula, includes the barren, volcanic landscape of the Valley of the Ten Thousand Smokes, Mount Katmai and Novarupta volcanoes, and the country's largest grizzly bear sanctuary.

*Malaspina Glacier,* near Yakutat, is North America's largest glacier.

*Misty Fiords National Monument,* near Ketchikan, features haunting fjords and a wildlife sanctuary.

*Pribilof Islands*, in the Bering Sea, are Aleut settlements whose rocky cliffs harbor colonies of fur seals and about two hundred species of seabirds, including puffins.

*Prince of Wales Island*, a ferry ride from Ketchikan, has abundant marine life and, at the Indian villages of Hydaburg and Klawock, fascinating totem parks.

*Prince William Sound*, southeast of Anchorage, is a natural wonderland of seals, whales, and other marine animals, as well as glaciers, fjords, and islands.

*Saint Nicholas Russian Orthodox Church*, in Eklutna, has a hand-hewn prayer chapel surrounded by brightly colored Dena'ina spirit houses.

## IMPORTANT DATES

c. 33,000 B.C.-21,000 B.C.—Paleo-Indians begin migrations across the Bering Land Bridge from Siberia into what is now Alaska and spread south across the Americas

c. 12,000 B.C.-7000 B.C.—Ancestors of Alaska's Athabascan Indians cross the Bering Land Bridge to Alaska

c. 7000 B.C.-4000 B.C.—Eskimos and Aleuts migrate to Alaska from Siberia and Arctic Canada

c. A.D. 1400-1700—Athabascan peoples spread to the North American Southwest and Great Plains regions

1724—Czar Peter the Great of Russia commissions Danish navigator Vitus Bering to explore the North Pacific region and see if Siberia and North America are connected

1728—Vitus Bering, exploring for Russia, passes Saint Lawrence Island and sails through what is now called the Bering Strait, between Alaska and Siberia

1741—Bering and Aleksey Chirikov sail toward the Alaskan coast; Chirikov's crew members approach land on Alaska's southeast coast; Bering's party lands on Kayak Island, becoming the first Europeans known to walk on Alaskan soil

1742—Bering dies on what is now called Bering Island; his crewmen return to Russia with hundreds of fur pelts, motivating fur traders to begin exploiting Alaska's fur-bearing animal resources

1743—Russians begin hunting Alaskan sea otters

1773—Juan Perez, sailing for Spain in the *Santiago*, reaches Alaska's southern coast

1775—Captain Juan Francisco de la Bodega y Quadra, sailing in the *Sonora*, lands near Sitka and claims Alaska's southern coast for Spain

1778—Captain James Cook surveys the Alaskan coast for Britain, exploring as far north as the Bering Strait

1779—A Spanish expedition reaches Bucareli Bay and sails along Alaska's coast as far as Cook Inlet

1784—Fur trader Grigory Shelikhov establishes the Russians' first permanent Alaskan settlement at Three Saints Bay on Kodiak Island

1786—Frenchman Jean François Galaup, Count Pérouse, lands at Liturga Bay while on a scientific exploration

1789—Spain seizes the British post at Nootka Sound

1792—Spain surrenders to British forces at Nootka Sound and loses all its claims to Alaskan land

1793—British explorer George Vancouver begins surveying Alaska's coast

1799—The Russian-American Company, with Aleksandr Baranov as manager, receives a twenty-year charter to trade in Russian America; the company establishes a post near Sitka

1802—Native Tlingits attack the Russian settlement at Sitka, killing a great number of Russians and their Aleut slaves

1804—The Russians retaliate against the Tlingit attack at Sitka, driving the Indians out of the area; Baranov rebuilds the Russian settlement, naming it New Archangel

1805—New Archangel (Sitka) becomes Russian America's seat of government

1821—Russia bars other countries from trading in Alaskan waters

1824—By a treaty with the United States, Alaska's southern boundary is set at the 54° 40′ latitude

1825—Alaska enters into a treaty with Great Britain, establishing boundaries and fishing rights; by a treaty, Canada and the United States agree on their mutual borders

1840—The Hudson's Bay Company, a British trading company, leases the southeastern Alaskan mainland from the Russians and establishes two trading posts

1847—The Hudson's Bay Company establishes Fort Yukon

1853—Oil is first observed in Cook Inlet

1857—Coal mining begins at Coal Harbor on the Kenai Peninsula

1867—In March, the United States purchases Alaska from Russia for $7.2 million in gold; the formal transfer ceremony is held in Sitka in October

1867-77—The U.S. Army governs Alaska

1868—Alaska's first newspaper, the *Sitka Times*, begins publication

1872—Gold is discovered near Sitka

1878—Alaska's first salmon canneries are built in Klawock and Sitka

1879—The U.S. Navy governs Alaska

1880—Gold is discovered in the Gastineau Channel area; due to gold-mining activity, Juneau, Douglas, and Treadwell are built

1884—By the Organic Act of 1884, Congress extends the laws of the state of Oregon to Alaska and creates an Alaskan federal court district, a land district, and an administrative system

1887—Anglican minister William Duncan leads Tsimshians from British Columbia to settle at Metlakatla on Annette Island

1896—Gold is discovered in the Klondike region of Canada's Yukon Territory; as prospectors rush to the Klondike, Alaskan towns along the gold-rush trail grow and prosper

1899—Gold is discovered in Nome; Alaska's own gold rush begins; Congress provides Alaska with a criminal-law code

1900—Alaska receives a civil-law code from Congress

1902—Felix Pedro discovers gold near Fairbanks

1903—Congress passes a homestead act for Alaska; an international commission settles a boundary dispute between Canada and the United States, establishing Canada's southwest seacoast at the 54° 40' latitude and its northwest seacoast at the head of the Portland Canal

1906—Alaska elects Frank H. Waskey as its first delegate to the U.S. Congress

1910—The Ballinger-Pinchot Affair over the use of national forestland containing coal draws attention to Alaska

1911—Copper production starts at Kennecott

**Douglas, a gold-mining town that once was larger than Juneau, was built in 1880.**

1912 — In the Second Organic Act, Congress declares Alaska a U.S. territory

1913 — Alaska's first territorial legislature convenes

1916 — An Alaska statehood bill is introduced in Congress but receives no hearing

1917 — Land is reserved near Fairbanks for the future University of Alaska

1922 — Alaska's first pulp mill opens at Speel River near Juneau

1923 — The Alaska Railroad, between Seward-Anchorage and Fairbanks, is completed

1935 — The Matanuska Valley Project begins, relocating farm families from the U.S. Midwest to Alaska

1942 — The Alaska Highway is built as a military supply route; the Japanese bomb Dutch Harbor in the Aleutian Islands and occupy Attu and Kiska islands

1943 — U.S. troops recapture occupied Alaskan territory from the Japanese

1953 — An oil well is drilled near Eureka; a pulp mill opens in Ketchikan

1956 — Alaska adopts its present constitution

**Benny Benson, who designed the Alaska flag when he was thirteen years old, poses with Governor William Egan in 1959, the year of Alaska's statehood.**

1957 — Oil is discovered in the Kenai Peninsula-Cook Inlet area

1958 — Congress votes to admit Alaska to the Union; Alaska holds its first state election, choosing state officials, two U.S. senators, and a U.S. representative

1959 — Alaska becomes the forty-ninth state on January 3

1963 — Alaska's Marine Highway system of ferries begins operation between cities in the southeast

1964 — North America's biggest earthquake devastates Valdez and the Anchorage area; the state's ferry system expands to include Kodiak Island and Prince William Sound

1965 — Alaska's state senate is reapportioned to provide representation based on population

1967 — Fairbanks suffers the worst flood in its history

1968 — Large oil reserves are discovered at Prudhoe Bay

1969 — Alaska auctions oil and gas leases on the Prudhoe Bay oil field

1971—The Alaska Native Claims Settlement Act (ANCSA) assigns 44 million acres (18 million hectares) of Alaskan land and $962.5 million to Alaska's native peoples

1972—Alaska's supreme court orders both houses of the state legislature to be reapportioned

1973—The Iditarod Trail Sled Dog Race begins its annual run

1974—Alyeska Pipeline Service Company begins construction of an oil pipeline from Prudhoe Bay to the port of Valdez on the Gulf of Alaska

1976—The Magnuson Act is passed, transferring fishing rights in Alaska's Exclusive Economic Zone to the United States beginning in 1978; the Molly Hootch Decree provides for secondary schools in all Alaskan communities; Alaskans vote to move the state capital from Juneau to Willow; the legislature establishes the Permanent Fund, designating state oil revenues to be divided among Alaska's residents

1977—The Trans-Alaska Pipeline, extending from Prudhoe Bay to Valdez, is completed; oil production at Prudhoe Bay begins

1978—Over 58 million acres (23 million hectares) of federal lands in Alaska are declared national monuments

1979—Due to high state revenues from oil, Alaska's legislature abolishes the state individual income tax

1980—The Alaska National Interest Lands Conservation Act (ANILCA) assigns 104 million acres (42 million hectares) of Alaskan land to the National Park System

1981—The state legislature is reapportioned once again

1982—Funding to move the state capital from Juneau to Willow is denied; the first Permanent Fund dividends are distributed

1985—A drop in world oil prices leads to a decline in Alaska's economy; Libby Riddles is the first woman to win the Iditarod race

1988—Vern Tejas makes the first successful solo winter climb of Mount McKinley

1989—The tanker *Exxon Valdez* runs aground in Prince William Sound, spilling 11 million gallons (42 million liters) of crude oil; massive cleanup efforts follow

1991—Alaska's Eskimos and Indians are entitled to begin selling or trading stock in native corporations holding lands awarded in the Alaska Native Claims Settlement Act

# IMPORTANT PEOPLE

**Clarence L. Andrews** (1862-1948), writer and newspaper publisher; lived in Alaska periodically from 1897; deputy collector of customs at Sitka, Skagway, and Eagle (1897-1909); did newspaper work in Alaska (1914-16); led a campaign to protect Eskimo-owned reindeer herds (1929-45); published *The Eskimo*, a quarterly paper devoted to Eskimo causes; wrote several books about Alaska, including *The Story of Sitka* (1922) and *The Story of Alaska* (1931)

**Aleksandr Andreyevich Baranov** (1746-1819), Russian fur trader; traveled to Alaska in 1790; general manager of the Russian-American Company (1799-1818); the first governor of Russian America; founded New Archangel, later renamed Sitka (1799)

**ALEKSANDR BARANOV**

**Edward Lewis Bartlett** (1904-1968), politician; lived in Alaska from the age of one; worked as a newspaper reporter and gold miner in Fairbanks; was elected Alaska's territorial representative to Congress (1944); actively campaigned for Alaska statehood; seated as U.S. senator from Alaska in 1959, the year of statehood, and was reelected twice; his statue represents Alaska in the U.S. Capitol in Washington, D.C.

**Vitus Jonassen Bering** (1681-1741), Danish navigator; sent by Czar Peter the Great of Russia to see if Asia and North America were connected by land (1725); sailed through the Bering Strait (1728); on second voyage (1741), explored Alaska's coast, discovered the Aleutian Islands, observed Mount Saint Elias, and landed on Kayak Island

**EDWARD BARTLETT**

**Charles Ernest Bunnell** (1878-1956), educator; came to Alaska in 1900 as a schoolteacher; principal of Valdez public schools; U.S. district judge in Alaska (1915-21); first president of Alaska Agricultural College and School of Mines, now the University of Alaska (1921-35); president of the University of Alaska (1935-49)

**Aleksey Chirikov** (1703-1748), Russian explorer; as captain of the *Saint Paul*, sailed on Vitus Bering's second expedition; his men were the first Europeans to sight Alaska, on July 15, 1741

**James Cook** (1728-1779), British explorer; led many voyages of discovery in the South Pacific; discovered Australia, New Zealand, and New Guinea; on his last expedition (1778), mapped the Pacific Coast of North America as far north as the Bering Strait

**VITUS BERING**

**WILLIAM DUNCAN**

**WILLIAM EGAN**

**WALTER HICKEL**

**JOSEPH JUNEAU**

**Anthony Joseph Dimond** (1881-1953), politician; came to Alaska as a prospector and miner (1904-12); mayor of Valdez (1920-22, 1925-32); member of Alaska's territorial senate (1923, 1925, 1929, 1931); Alaska's territorial representative to the U.S. Congress (1933-45); U.S. district judge in Anchorage (1945-53)

**William Duncan** (1832-1918), Anglican minister; in 1887, led a group of Tsimshian Indians from British Columbia to settle at Metlakatla on Annette Island

**William Allen Egan** (1914-1984), born in Valdez; politician; member of Alaska's territorial legislature (1941-55); chairman of Alaska's constitutional convention (1955-56); as Tennessee Plan senator (1956-58), worked to promote Alaska statehood; the first governor of the state of Alaska (1959-66, 1970-74)

**Carl Ben Eielson** (1897-1929), aviator; bush pilot who developed commercial airplane flying in Alaska in the 1920s

**Ernest Gruening** (1887-1974), politician, journalist; on staff of the U.S. Department of the Interior (1934-39); member of the Alaska International Highway Commission (1938-42); governor of territorial Alaska (1939-53); U.S. senator from Alaska (1959-69); author of several books, including *The State of Alaska* (1954), *An Alaskan Reader* (1961), and *The Battle for Alaska Statehood* (1967)

**William McKendree Gwin** (1805-1885), political leader; U.S. senator from California (1850-55, 1857-61); campaigned for the purchase of Alaska, partly to extend Californians' fishing rights northward

**B. Frank Heintzleman** (1888-1965), forester, territorial governor; came to Alaska on staff of U.S. Forest Service (1918-34); regional forester for Alaska (1937-53); territorial governor of Alaska (1953-57)

**Walter Joseph Hickel** (1919-     ), business executive, politician; builder-owner of investment company in Anchorage (1947-   ); builder-owner of motels, hotels, and shopping centers in Anchorage and Fairbanks (1953-82); governor of Alaska (1966-69); U.S. secretary of the interior (1969-70)

**Sheldon Jackson** (1834-1909), educator, missionary; came to Alaska in 1884 to establish a Presbyterian mission; instigated a conference to divide Alaska among the various Protestant denominations; Alaska's superintendent of public instruction (1885-1908); opened many free schools for Eskimos; a sponsor of the Sitka Industrial School, since renamed Sheldon Jackson College

**Joseph Juneau** (1826?-1900), prospector and gold miner; with fellow prospector Richard Harris and three Tlingit Indians, discovered gold near present-day Juneau in 1880, touching off the Alaska gold rush; the resulting boomtown of Juneau was named after him

**Austin Eugene Lathrop** (1865-1950), industrialist; in 1896, expanded his Seattle business enterprises to Alaska, engaging in transportation, coal and gold mining, theater, radio, and newspaper businesses; Alaska's first millionaire industrial giant

**Sydney Laurence** (1865-1939), artist; painted Alaskan landscapes and other local scenery

**John Muir** (1838-1914), naturalist, conservationist; toured much of the United States studying botanical specimens; studied plants of Alaska in the 1870s; campaigned to establish Yosemite National Park and to save U.S. forest reserves; influenced President Theodore Roosevelt in setting aside land for national forests, including forestland in Alaska; his many books include *Travels in Alaska* (1915)

**Felix Pedro** (1859?-1910), born Felice Pedroni in Italy; prospector and gold miner throughout the American West and Pacific Northwest; discovered gold near Fairbanks in 1902

**Jean François Galaup, Count Pérouse** (1741-1788), French explorer; sighted Alaska's southern coast in 1786 during a scientific expedition to the American Northwest

**Peter (the Great) Alekseyevich** (1672-1725), czar of Russia (1682-1725); founded Saint Petersburg as the new Russian capital (1703); reorganized Russian government and military and established Russia's first navy; brought in western European ideas and customs and raised Russia to the status of a major European power; before his death, he commissioned Vitus Bering to explore the North Pacific Ocean to see if Asia and North America were connected by land; these explorations led to the discovery of Alaska

**Peter Trimble Rowe** (1856-1942), clergyman; was appointed Alaska's first Episcopal bishop (1894)

**Robert William Service** (1874-1958), poet; colorful resident of British Columbia and the Yukon Territory; traveled extensively in Alaska and the Yukon; recorded his experiences in ballads such as "The Shooting of Dan McGrew" and "The Cremation of Sam McGee"; his poetry collections include *Songs of a Sourdough* (1907) and *Trail of '98* (1909)

**William Henry Seward** (1801-1872), politician; governor of New York (1839-43); leader of the antislavery Whig party; U.S. senator from Alaska (1849-61); as U.S. secretary of state (1861-69), arranged for the purchase of Alaska from Russia in 1867

**Grigory Ivanovich Shelikhov** (1747-1795), Russian merchant and fur trader; as a leader of the Shelikhov-Golikov Company, organized a trading expedition to Alaska (1783); founded Russia's first permanent settlement in Alaska, at Three Saints Bay on Kodiak Island (1784); after his death, his company formed the basis of the Russian-American Company

**AUSTIN LATHROP**

**JOHN MUIR**

**COUNT PÉROUSE**

**GRIGORY SHELIKHOV**

**THEODORE STEVENS**

**GEORGE VANCOUVER**

**SAMUEL YOUNG**

**Theodore Fulton Stevens** (1923-    ), lawyer, politician; U.S. Attorney for Alaska (1953-56); on staff of U.S. Department of the Interior (1956-60); practiced law in Anchorage (1961-64); member of Alaska's house of representatives (1964-68); U.S. senator from Alaska (1968-    ); Senate Republican whip (1977-85)

**George Vancouver** (1757-1798), British navigator; sailed around the world and to the Arctic with Captain James Cook; surveyed and mapped North America's west coast for the British navy, working as far north as Cook Inlet (1792-94); gave British names to many of Alaska's geographical features

**Ioann (Ivan) Veniaminov** (1797-1879), Russian Orthodox priest, scientist, and scholar; in 1824, he settled and taught on the Aleutian island of Unalaska, where he composed an Aleut dictionary and grammar; was appointed first Russian Orthodox bishop of Russian America (1840); opened the General College of the Russian Colony at New Archangel (1859)

**Frank Hinman Waskey** (1875-1964), politician; Alaska's first territorial representative to the U.S. Congress; elected in 1906, he was entitled to speak, but not vote, in the House of Representatives

**James Wickersham** (1857-1939), judge and politician; came to Alaska in 1900; U.S. district judge in Alaska (1900-07); Alaska's territorial representative to the U.S. Congress (1909-21, 1931-33); introduced Alaska's first statehood enabling bill to Congress (1916)

**Samuel Hall Young** (1847-1927), Presbyterian missionary, explorer; came to Alaska in 1878 as a missionary to Fort Wrangell; founded Alaska's first Protestant church (1879); organized missions at Eagle and Rampart (1899) and at Nome and Teller (1900); by dog team and boat, traveled extensively throughout Alaska and the Siberian coast; explored Glacier Bay with John Muir and discovered Muir Glacier (1880)

## GOVERNORS

| | | | |
|---|---|---|---|
| William A. Egan | 1959-1966 | William J. Sheffield | 1982-1986 |
| Walter J. Hickel | 1966-1969 | Steve Cowper | 1986- |
| Keith H. Miller | 1969-1970 | | |
| William A. Egan | 1970-1974 | | |
| Jay S. Hammond | 1974-1982 | | |

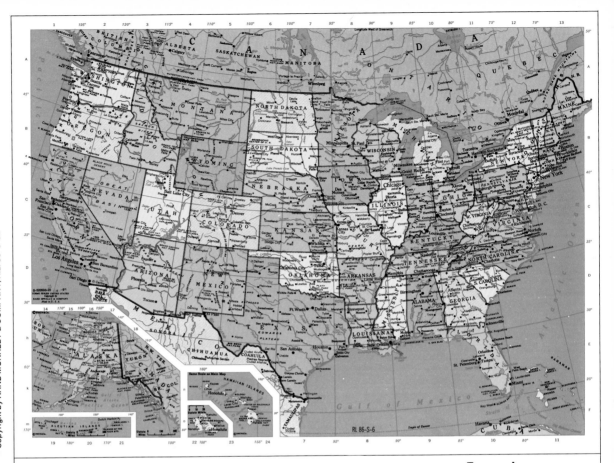

RL 86-S-6

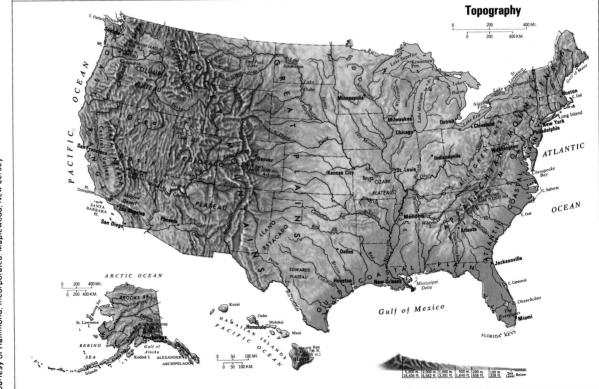

**Topography**

0        200        400 MI.

0        200        400 KM.

PACIFIC OCEAN

ATLANTIC OCEAN

Gulf of Mexico

ARCTIC OCEAN

0    200    400 MI.

0    200    400 KM.

BERING SEA

Gulf of Alaska

ALEXANDER ARCHIPELAGO

HAWAIIAN ISLANDS

PACIFIC OCEAN

0    50    100 MI.

0    50    100 KM.

| 5,000 m. | 2,000 m. | 1,000 m. | 500 m. | 200 m. | 100 m. | Sea Level |
|----------|----------|----------|--------|--------|--------|-----------|
| 16,404 ft. | 6,562 ft. | 3,281 ft. | 1,640 ft. | 656 ft. | 328 ft. | Below |

## MAP KEY

From *Cosmopolitan World Atlas* © 1990 by Rand McNally, R.L. 90-S-87

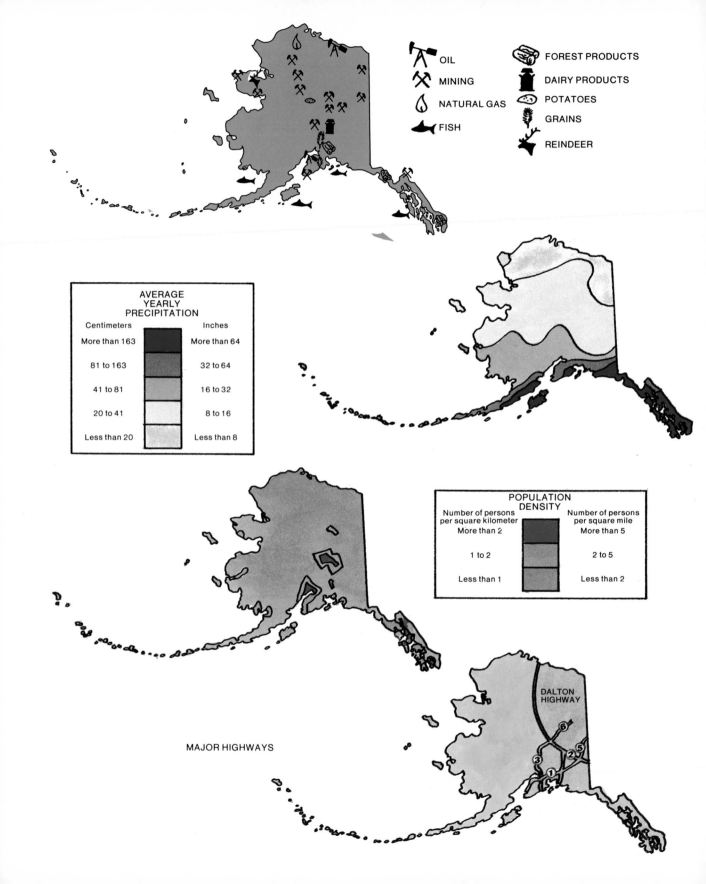

OIL

MINING

NATURAL GAS

FISH

FOREST PRODUCTS

DAIRY PRODUCTS

POTATOES

GRAINS

REINDEER

AVERAGE YEARLY PRECIPITATION

| Centimeters | | Inches |
|---|---|---|
| More than 163 | | More than 64 |
| 81 to 163 | | 32 to 64 |
| 41 to 81 | | 16 to 32 |
| 20 to 41 | | 8 to 16 |
| Less than 20 | | Less than 8 |

POPULATION DENSITY

| Number of persons per square kilometer | | Number of persons per square mile |
|---|---|---|
| More than 2 | | More than 5 |
| 1 to 2 | | 2 to 5 |
| Less than 1 | | Less than 2 |

MAJOR HIGHWAYS

DALTON HIGHWAY

TOPOGRAPHY

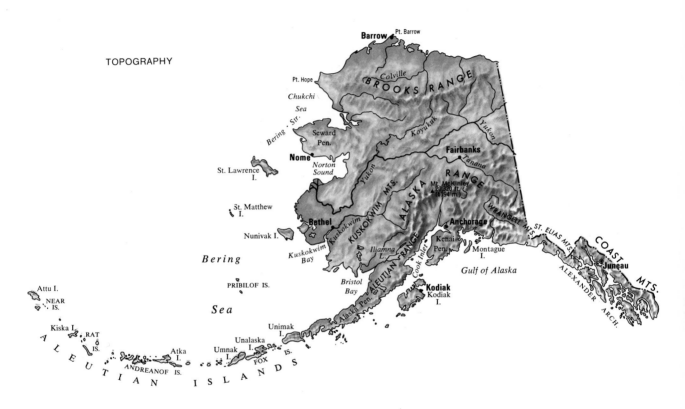

Pt. Barrow
**Barrow**
Colville
BROOKS RANGE
Pt. Hope
*Chukchi*
*Sea*
*Bering · Str.*
Seward
Pen.
**Nome**
*Norton*
*Sound*
Koyukuk
Yukon
St. Lawrence
I.
Yukon
**Fairbanks**
*Tanana*
ALASKA RANGE
St. Matthew
I.
KUSKOKWIM MTS.
Mt. McKinley
20,320 ft.
(6194 m.)
WRANGELL MTS.
**Bethel**
**Anchorage**
Nunivak I.
Kuskokwim
*Iliamna*
*L.*
Kenai
Pen.
Montague
I.
ST. ELIAS MTS.
COAST
*Bering*
Kuskokwim
Bay
*Cook Inlet*
*Gulf of Alaska*
**Juneau**
MTS.
Attu I.
NEAR
IS.
*Sea*
PRIBILOF IS.
ALEUTIAN RANGE
ALEXANDER
ARCH.
Kiska I.
RAT
IS.
Atka
I.
Umnak
I.
Unalaska
I.
Unimak
I.
Alaska Pen.
*Bristol*
*Bay*
**Kodiak**
Kodiak
I.
ALEUTIAN ISLANDS
ANDREANOF IS.
FOX
IS.

Below Sea
Level | 100 m.
328 ft. | 200 m.
656 ft. | 500 m.
1,640 ft. | 1,000 m.
3,281 ft. | 2,000 m.
6,562 ft. | 5,000 m.
16,404 ft.

Courtesy of Hammond, Incorporated
Maplewood, New Jersey

The Aleutian Island
of Unalaska, near
Dutch Harbor

# INDEX

Page numbers that appear in boldface type indicate illustrations

**The Chugach Mountains form a backdrop for these small planes lined up on an airfield.**

**Kenai Fjords
National Park, on
Kenai Peninsula**

**Picture Identifications**

**Front cover:** Misty Fiords National Monument, in southeast Alaska
**Back cover:** Autumn colors blanket the tundra in Denali National Park
**Pages 2-3:** A musher and his dog team on the Iditarod Trail, near Nome
**Page 6:** Blueberry Lake, east of Valdez
**Pages 8-9:** Mount McKinley
**Pages 24-25:** Montage of Alaskans
**Page 32:** The midnight sun at Kotzebue
**Pages 46-47:** Miners prospecting for gold near Fairbanks in 1905
**Page 56:** The Trans-Alaska Pipeline
**Page 64:** Boats in the harbor at Valdez
**Pages 78-79:** Climbers on Mount McKinley
**Pages 90-91:** Anchorage
**Page 108:** Montage showing the state flag, state tree (Sitka spruce), state bird (willow ptarmigan), state mineral (gold), and state flower (forget-me-not)

## About the Author

Ann Heinrichs is a free-lance writer and editor living in Chicago. She has worked for such educational publishers as Encyclopaedia Britannica, World Book Encyclopedia, and Science Research Associates. As a music critic and feature writer, her articles have appeared in various publications. She is the author of a number of books, including several in the *America the Beautiful* series.

## Picture Acknowledgments

Front cover, © **Joan Dunlop;** 2-3, **SuperStock;** 4, © **Kirkendall/Spring;** 5, **SuperStock;** 6, © Fred Chapman/**Root Resources;** 8-9, © Sharon Cummings/**M.L. Dembinsky, Jr., Photography Associates;** 11, © Phil Degginger/**TSW-Click/Chicago Ltd.;** 12, © **Bob Willis;** 15, © **Bob & Ira Spring;** 16, © **Jeff Schultz Photography;** 17 (left), **map art by Len Meents;** 17 (right), © Stephen J. Krasemann/**Valan Photos;** 18 (top left), © **Bob & Ira Spring;** 18 (top right), © Sharon Cummings/**M.L. Dembinsky, Jr., Photography Associates;** 18 (bottom left), © John Shaw/**Tom Stack & Associates;** 18 (bottom right), © **Jeff Schultz Photography;** 21, © **Jeff Schultz Photography;** 23 (left), **Photri;** 23 (right), © **Bob & Ira Spring;** 24 (top left), © **Bob & Ira Spring;** 24 (top right), © **Joan Dunlop;** 24 (bottom left), © **Jeff Schultz Photography;** 24 (bottom right), © E. Herwig/**Marilyn Gartman Agency;** 25 (top left, middle right, and bottom left), © **Bob & Ira Spring;** 25 (middle left), © **Jeff Schultz Photography;** 25 (bottom right), © **Buddy Mays;** 28 (left), © **Porterfield/Chickering;** 28 (right), © **Bob & Ira Spring;** 32, © **Joan Dunlop;** 34 (left), **Photri;** 34 (right), **Alaska & Polar Regions Department, Elmer E. Rasmuson Library, University of Alaska Fairbanks, Charles Bunnell Collection;** 35, **Alaska & Polar Regions Department, Elmer E. Rasmuson Library, University of Alaska Fairbanks, Albert Johnson Collection;** 38, © **Bob & Ira Spring;** 40 (left), **Historical Pictures Service, Chicago;** 40 (right), **AP/Wide World Photos;** 41, **Alaska & Polar Regions Department, Elmer E. Rasmuson Library, University of Alaska Fairbanks, B. Willoughby Collection;** 43, **Historical Pictures Service, Chicago;** 44, **Laurie Platt Winfrey, Inc.;** 45, **Historical Pictures Service, Chicago;** 46-47, **Alaska & Polar Regions Department, Elmer E. Rasmuson Library, University of Alaska Fairbanks, Ralph Mackay Collection;** 49, **Alaska & Polar Regions Department, Elmer E. Rasmuson Library, University of Alaska Fairbanks, Historical Photograph Collection;** 50, **Alaska & Polar Regions Department, Elmer E. Rasmuson Library, University of Alaska Fairbanks, Charles Bunnell Collection;** 51, **Alaska & Polar Regions Department, Elmer E. Rasmuson Library, University of Alaska Fairbanks, Historical Photograph Collection;** 52, **Alaska & Polar Regions Department, Elmer E. Rasmuson Library, University of Alaska Fairbanks, Fairbanks Collection;** 53, **Alaska & Polar Regions Department, Elmer E. Rasmuson Library, University of Alaska Fairbanks, Hanna Collection;** 55, **AP/Wide World Photos;** 56, © Vince Streano/**TSW-Click/Chicago Ltd.;** 58, **AP/Wide World Photos;** 60, © **Cameramann International Ltd.;** 63, © Rob Stapleton/**M.L. Dembinsky, Jr., Photography Associates;** 64, © Sharon Cummings/**M.L. Dembinsky, Jr., Photography Associates;** 67, © **Porterfield/Chickering;** 68, © Lael Morgan/**TSW-Click/Chicago Ltd.;** 70 (left), © Mark Reinholz/**Marilyn Gartman Agency;** 70 (right), © **Porterfield/Chickering;** 71, © **Porterfield/Chickering;** 73 (left), © Phil Degginger/**TSW-Click/Chicago Ltd.;** 73 (right), © **Bob & Ira Spring;** 75, © Lael Morgan/**TSW-Click/Chicago Ltd.;** 76, © **Bob & Ira Spring;** 77, © Nancy Boyd Johnson/**Photo Options;** 78-79, © Rob Stapleton/**M.L. Dembinsky, Jr., Photography Associates;** 82 (both pictures), © Susan Braine/**M.L. Dembinsky, Jr., Photography Associates;** 85, © **Bob & Ira Spring;** 87 (top left, top right, and bottom left), © Atchison/**Photri;** 87 (bottom right), © **Bob & Ira Spring;** 89, © **Bob & Ira Spring;** 90-91, © John W. Warden/**SuperStock;** 93, © **Bob & Ira Spring;** 94 (maps), **Len Meents;** 94 (right), © **Jeff Schultz Photography;** 95, © **Bob & Ira Spring;** 96, © **Bob & Ira Spring;** 97 (left), © **Jeff Schultz Photography;** 97 (right), © **Porterfield/Chickering;** 98 (maps), **Len Meents;** 98 (right), © **Joan Dunlop;** 100, © T. Lemke/**Third Coast Stock Source;** 101, © **Jeff Schultz Photography;** 102 (maps), **Len Meents;** 102 (right), © K. Scholz/**H. Armstrong Roberts;** 104 (map), **Len Meents;** 104 (right), © Nancy Boyd Johnson/**Photo Options;** 107 (left), © **Jeff Schultz Photography;** 107 (map), **Len Meents;** 108 (background), © **Jeff Schultz Photography;** 108 (flower), © **Bob & Ira Spring;** 108 (gold), **Photri;** 108 (bird), © Sharon Cummings/**M.L. Dembinsky, Jr., Photography Associates;** 108 (flag), **Courtesy Flag Research Center, Winchester, Massachusetts 01890;** 112, © Wes Bergen/**Root Resources;** 114 (both pictures), © Tom Ulrich/**TSW-Click/Chicago Ltd.;** 119 (both pictures), © **Bob & Ira Spring;** 122, © Eugene G. Schulz/**Third Coast Stock Source;** 126, **Alaska & Polar Regions Department, Elmer E. Rasmuson Library, University of Alaska Fairbanks, Historical Photograph Collection;** 127, **Alaska & Polar Regions Department, Elmer E. Rasmuson Library, University of Alaska Fairbanks, W. Egan Collection;** 129 (top and bottom), **Historical Pictures Service, Chicago;** 129 (middle), **AP/Wide World Photos;** 130 (Duncan and Egan), **AP/Wide World Photos;** 130 (Hickel and Juneau), **Historical Pictures Service, Chicago;** 131 (top), **AP/Wide World Photos;** 131 (Muir, La Pérouse, and Shelikhov), **Historical Pictures Service, Chicago;** 132 (top), **AP/Wide World Photos;** 132 (middle and bottom), **Historical Pictures Service, Chicago;** 138, **Shostal/SuperStock;** 141, © John W. Warden/**SuperStock;** 143, © Rob Stapleton/**M.L. Dembinsky, Jr., Photography Associates;** back cover, © **Lynn M. Stone**